AF386546

Success through Cooperation

Success through Cooperation

The First Decade of the GPCA, 2006–2015

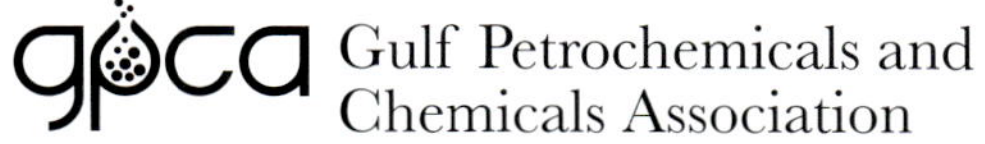

Printed in Dubai, United Arab Emirates

ISBN: 978-1-909339-79-8 Hardback
ISBN: 978-1-909339-80-4 Softback

Book design by Mark Willie Graphic Design
Published by Medina Publishing Ltd., UK

Contents

Map of Gulf Cooperation Council Countries   vi

Foreword   vii

Preface   ix

Introduction   xi

Chapter 1: **Planting the Seed**   1

Chapter 2: **Birth of the GPCA**   7

Chapter 3: **Developing Capacity, Expanding Benefits, Growing Membership**   13

Chapter 4: **Working Committees**   29

Chapter 5: **The Annual Forum and Other Major Events**   43

Chapter 6: **The GPCA Today**   57

Appendix

Milestones: The GPCA's Journey   64

A Note on Sources   67

Map of Gulf Cooperation Council Countries

Foreword

Among the many signs of encouraging progress in our global life, one of the most surprising and impressive is the growth of modern industry in the six countries of the Gulf Cooperation Council, or GCC (Bahrain, Kuwait, Oman, Qatar, Saudi Arabia, and the United Arab Emirates). Long centuries ago, Arab pioneers dominated in the cultivation of the chemical sciences and technologies—a reality encapsulated in their development of the crucial art of distillation. (In medieval Europe, the still—the essential breakthrough technology—would long be known as "the moor's head.") However the industrial revolution and the rise of modern society passed the area by, leaving it characterized by splintered tribes and nations, illiteracy, and poverty.

The discovery and exploitation of oil in the first half of the twentieth century altered the picture somewhat, but even in the 1950s and 1960s it seemed that the Arab role would be limited to that of resource supplier. In 1965, no one was predicting that a mere half century later the GCC nations would be the home of a buoyant, expanding petrochemical industry supplying over 10 percent of world production by volume of an array of key chemicals. Downstream development and growth in global market share define the present agenda and the ventures that lie ahead for chemical manufacturers in the Arabian Gulf States.

Coordinating the activities of the many players within the burgeoning chemical sector is the job of the Gulf Petrochemicals and Chemicals Association (GPCA). In its first short decade of existence, GPCA (founded March 2006) has grown to be a major, perhaps the single most important, port of call for global leaders in petrochemicals. In particular, the GPCA Annual Forum in November each year is where those leaders gather to exchange views, appraise challenges, and assess the opportunities that lie ahead.

The GPCA itself has made the enlightened decision to produce two books to celebrate its first decade. This present account, *Success through Cooperation*, details the origin, growth, and functions of the GPCA itself. It offers an encouraging chronicle of progress made and challenges met. It is also an implicit promise of further progress in the decade ahead. The second publication has both a larger time frame and a more complex story. *Molecules, Mind, and Matter* covers the half century in which a major industry was developed from scratch. That industry simultaneously provides rewarding employment for tens of thousands of GCC citizens, creates ever more valuable and sophisticated products, and supplies a steadily growing world demand.

The progress and promise of science and industry in the GCC is a story of courage, inventiveness, and vision. It is a pleasure to commend it to you as an antidote to a world too often beset by rancor, gloom, and human folly.

Arnold Thackray
Chancellor, Chemical Heritage Foundation

Preface

The publication of this account of the first decade of the Gulf Petrochemicals and Chemicals Association (GPCA) coincides with the tenth Annual GPCA Forum in November 2015. This book appears just before the GPCA's tenth anniversary itself, which will be celebrated during the association's Annual General Meeting in March 2016. At that time, we shall be recalling our proud record over the past decade as well as looking forward to the challenges that lie ahead.

While the petrochemical industry in the Arabian Gulf region dates back to the mid-1960s, it was not until the early 2000s that a platform representing common industry interests was officially launched. The establishment of the GPCA, as the voice of the chemical industry in the Gulf Cooperation Council (GCC), was driven by the wisdom of the GPCA's eight visionary founding members, represented by the CEOs of the leading petrochemical producers who ensured that the concept would become a reality, and by the vast expansion of regional chemical players, which created the necessary critical mass for launching a platform for knowledge sharing and the exchange of best practices.

Since our establishment in 2006, we have built a remarkable reputation and image. We have consistently expanded the association's membership. Launched with just over 60 members, total membership of the GPCA now stands at 240, making the founding members' vision of steering the regional industry toward a whole new level of collaboration a reality.

As you read this book, you will realize how our networking, thought leadership, and advocacy initiatives have helped our members to connect, to share and advance knowledge, and to contribute to international dialogue. You will also realize that it is not only a history of achievements and successes, but that challenges and sometimes setbacks are also part of our story.

It has very much been a journey, one that would not have been possible without the guidance of our Board of Directors and the strong support and dedication of our members, whose thoughts, decisions, and actions have determined not only the policies, direction, and development of the GPCA but also have had a crucial impact on building the GPCA into the most successful trade association in the region.

We are very grateful to our past and current committee members and to their companies that have delegated key personnel to be part of the GPCA structure. In addition, we thank our peer associations in North America and Europe for their continued support and sharing of experience and best practices. Finally, this journey would not have been the same without the Secretariat's staff that joined us along the way.

With this and with the inherent strengths of our members, we can be confident that the chemical industry in the GCC, and this association, will prevail and gain even greater heights of prosperity and accomplishments in the future.

Abdulwahab Al-Sadoun
Secretary General, Gulf Petrochemicals and Chemicals Association

Introduction

A new era for the petrochemical industry began late in the twentieth century. Arabian Gulf nations were seeking ways to extract more value from the abundant hydrocarbon resources that lay beneath their land. At the same time, there were burgeoning markets for petrochemical products, especially in Asia. Also, high prices for energy and feedstock were turning the attention of Western chemical companies to fresh options. Increased revenue from higher oil prices enabled the governments of the GCC both to build world-class infrastructure and to finance capital-intensive petrochemical facilities. Bold movements by leaders in the Arabian Gulf region set the stage for the formation of the Gulf Petrochemicals and Chemicals Association (GPCA).

Initially, the only company in the region with large-scale petrochemical operations was Saudi Basic Industries Corporation (SABIC), founded in 1976. By the mid-1980s SABIC was manufacturing a broad range of products, including urea, ammonia, methanol, methyl tertiary butyl ether, ethylene, ethylene glycol, and high-density and low-density polyethylene. Other petrochemical enterprises in the region were much smaller in scale and, with the exception of Qatar Petrochemical Company (QAPCO), limited to methane-based products. By the early 2000s, ambitious projects had been launched in Qatar, Kuwait, Abu Dhabi, and Oman to construct large-scale manufacturing facilities for a much broader slate of chemicals. Simultaneously, in Saudi Arabia, SABIC continued to grow, while the private petrochemical sector also began to blossom.

The expanding companies in the Arabian Gulf region confronted a host of challenges connected with employee development, workplace safety, access to feedstock, environmental protection, community relations, logistics, and global marketing. As early as 2001, the enormity and scope of these challenges convinced a small cadre of individuals in Abu Dhabi, Bahrain, Kuwait, Qatar, and Saudi Arabia of the need for producers in the region to come together. Their desire was to share information and experience, organize workshops and other learning opportunities, gather industry data and make it available, and create a single voice to represent the Gulf petrochemical sector in the global arena. This desire spawned the formation of the GPCA and still guides it today.

Reflecting back on these beginnings, Maha Mulla Hussain, former managing director and chair of Kuwait's Petrochemical Industries Company (PIC), observed:

> The petrochemical industry in most Arabian Gulf countries at first was very limited. As companies began expanding at the end of the 1990s, and started looking globally, they came to understand that they needed to sit down together. In other regions, companies were talking to each other and exchanging views and best practices. We thought we too should learn from each other. After all, we were facing common challenges, challenges unique to our region.

Other early figures in the GPCA saw matters similarly. Hubert Puchner, former chief executive officer (CEO) of Abu Dhabi's Borouge, says,

> It was clear by 2000 that the center of gravity of the petrochemical industry was moving to the Middle East. We needed to create a regional organization that would promote the industry, customer care, the importance of quality, and the value of innovation.

What follows is the story of the origins of the GPCA, and of its development into a regional organization with global significance. It is an adventure story, inextricably linked to the astonishing reality of the emergence of a high-tech petrochemical industry amid the sands of the desert. It is, moreover, a story that has just begun.

1 Planting the Seed

Setting the Stage

In January 2001, at the MariChem conference in Dubai, the idea of creating an association of Arabian Gulf petrochemical producers was bruited about. Abdulrahman Jawahery, president of Bahrain's Gulf Petrochemical Industries Company (GPIC), remembers,

> We thought, "Why not share knowledge?" We were training people. We were exchanging technical information. We had the same culture. Instead of doing it haphazardly, why don't we create an organization that brings people together under one umbrella, so we can benefit from sharing safety, environmental, and technical experiences? And we should include people from abroad.

Maha Mulla Hussain points to Hamad Al-Terkait, former president and CEO of Kuwait's EQUATE Petrochemical Company, as a key advocate and an important driver in bringing to fruition the vision for a new association. Al-Terkait was, according to Hussain, "a vehicle for promoting the organization and for convincing others."

> He met with other CEOs from the Gulf at EPCA [European Petrochemical Association] meetings and elsewhere. He asked them, "Why don't we have something similar in the GCC [Gulf Cooperation Council] region? We are growing. We are influential." There was some resistance. He worked hand in hand with Hubert Puchner and Mohamed Al-Azdi of Borouge, Abdulrahman Jawahery of GPIC, and others: they had a mission and they succeeded.

Leaders from Abu Dhabi National Oil Company (ADNOC) and Borouge organized a meeting in 2003 in Dubai. That meeting brought together proponents like Al-Terkait and Jawahery and also representatives of QAPCO and PIC. However, Hubert Puchner notes how after the meeting everyone simply went back to their companies. There was no real follow-up until 2004, when Al-Terkait started calling for action. A second meeting was held in Kuwait, during which founding members "put together the constitution" for what would become known

> The GPCA is and will continue to be the umbrella organization for the Arabian Gulf chemical and petrochemical manufacturers. It is their sole and unique spokesman, speaking to the global chemical industry. The members and associates of the GPCA need to strengthen their communication and close cooperation to fulfill their role in service to the chemical community and the Arabian Gulf region. For that to happen, all of us in the industry must adopt the GPCA as our banner going into the future.
>
> *—Hamad Al-Terkait, founding vice chairman of GPCA and former CEO of EQUATE*

eventually as the Gulf Petrochemicals and Chemicals Association, or GPCA. Its gestation would prove lengthy: it was not until 2006 that the association was actually launched.

SABIC

In the Arabian Gulf States, producers from Abu Dhabi, Bahrain, Kuwait, and Qatar were agreed on the idea of a petrochemical association. In 2005, Saudi Arabia's Tasnee, a private petrochemical company, agreed it made sense to join in. "All of us felt that we needed to get together," says Moayyed Al-Qurtas, former CEO of Tasnee, who shares how Tasnee's marketing staff took the initiative and then proceeded to convince senior management.

The stumbling block to moving forward, however, was the reluctance of SABIC. There was unanimous agreement among the proponents of an association that SABIC's participation was crucial. SABIC's productive capacity was greater than that of all the other companies combined. Further, SABIC was already a significant player on the global scene. Its presence was essential if the attention and respect of the chemical industry was to be directed on the soon-to-be-born organization. According to Jawahery,

> We recognized that without the support of Saudi Arabia and specifically SABIC, we would not succeed. SABIC was one of the larger petrochemical companies in the world, and we needed its support.

Mohamed Al-Azdi, former CEO of Abu Dhabi National Chemical Company (ChemaWEyaat) believes that SABIC's reluctance was at least partly due to the issue of where the GPCA would be headquartered:

We think the issue of headquarters contributed to SABIC's hesitation. We said the headquarters for the regional chemical industry should be in Dubai because Dubai is neutral. It is not involved with oil and gas that much, and it has a very liberal set of laws and regulations relating to nonprofit organizations.

Al-Terkait was persistent in contacting SABIC. He made clear that those calling for the creation of an association would not go forward without SABIC: "An association without SABIC was no association. We hoped it would join." Still SABIC demurred. Al-Azdi recalls, "We insisted we could not start without SABIC, but it took us some time to convince them." At Tasnee, enthusiasm had come from the bottom reaches of the company. The opposite was true at SABIC, where "it took time for the proposal to reach the top. People at the lower levels didn't focus on it."

By spring 2005, representatives of several companies were becoming impatient and wished to create the GPCA without SABIC. Al-Terkait thought it worth one more effort to bring SABIC into the association. He wrote a personal letter to SABIC's then vice chairman and CEO, Mohamed Al-Mady, explaining that the new association was "nothing commercial; it's not a cartel." At the same time, Jawahery paid Al-Mady a visit.

He was kind enough to open his door for me and give me half an hour to explain what we wanted to achieve. He asked, "What is your plan? What is your vision?"

I told him, "We need to share information on safety, environment, health, training, and technical issues. I am one of the people whom SABIC trained twenty years ago. Why not support us in creating an organization that brings us together for such purposes? We are not talking about marketing or prices. We want an organization that will support the sustainability of our industry." I explained that without SABIC, we would not succeed.

Mohamed Al-Mady, CEO of SABIC in 2006, was the natural choice to serve as GPCA's first chairman.

Al-Mady responded positively. "Once the idea was in front of him, he grasped it and saw its potential," said Jawahery. Al-Mady discussed the issue with SABIC executives. He asked Homood Al-Tuwaijri, former vice president of petrochemicals coordination at SABIC, to call and accept. "He said Mr. Al-Mady will support it. SABIC was in."

"All were agreed that Al-Mady should chair the new organization, so we could get the full support of the Saudis," explains Jawahery. Moayyed Al-Qurtas, then CEO of Tasnee, who had worked with Al-Mady at SABIC, adds, "We were lucky that Mr. Al-Mady agreed to be the founding chairman. He utilized all his international relationships to give the GPCA status." Al-Terkait also agreed it was essential that Al-Mady take the lead role.

Al-Terkait became the vice chairman. Though it was initially agreed that Al-Terkait would become chair after Al-Mady's term came to an end, when that time came, Al-Terkait declined to take the chairmanship:

> I said, "Let's have the big guys, the biggest brother in the lead." This gives us global leverage because when we send letters out from the GPCA, so many people listen because of SABIC's size. We can utilize the image.
>
> When it came to reelection time, I told the board, "I don't want to bid for chairmanship. We are all together working for the success. We are not concerned with who's taking which title or who runs what. No, we are behind the GPCA flag. It represents all of us, and this is what is most important."

A Common Platform

In early June 2005, the fledgling Gulf association was ready to launch. Two hundred top executives, representing every major international plastics and

The GPCA has helped the chemical community in so many ways. It has consolidated the Arabian Gulf chemicals industry; it has helped increase global understanding of the role and purpose of the chemical industry in our region; it has championed concern about the environment while strengthening the readiness of the chemical industry to meet global demand. It has played an essential role, far more than we dreamed when we created this wonderful organization.

—Mohamed Al-Azdi, former CEO, ChemaWEyaat

petrochemicals corporation in the world, arrived in Bahrain to attend the Middle East Economic Digest's (MEED) Gulf Petrochemicals Conference.

Al-Terkait confirmed to delegates that plans to establish the new association were moving ahead. Creation was expected "by the end of the year." The association would model itself on the EPCA. It would be a nonprofit organization, likely based in Dubai, created to facilitate the exchange of information and experiences among petrochemical companies, creating a "data bank" and other technical assistance and resources.

Al-Terkait, Jawahery, Puchner, and other key players planned to recruit Gulf-based producers with a capacity of more than a hundred thousand tons. They thought that later on, the new association would look "to invite Egypt, Iraq, and other regional countries into the fold." The EPCA would be an honorary member, while downstream companies could become associate members.

The effort to create an association of Arabian Gulf petrochemical producers had come to fruition at last. Members of the association would tackle challenges together, membership would grow, and the association would enable the Gulf's voice to be heard around the world.

2 Birth of the GPCA

A Formal Structure

On 1 March 2006, the CEOs of eight petrochemical companies—SABIC, Tasnee, EQUATE, PIC, GPIC, Borouge, QAPCO, and Qatar Vinyl Company (QVC)—came together to establish the Gulf Petrochemicals and Chemicals Association. The eight companies become known as the Founding Members.

The initial board of the GPCA consisted of the eight leaders of the founding companies, though it was recognized that more members might be added. The organization's articles of association called for an annual general assembly to elect and appoint directors as appropriate, determine fees, and approve accounts; a secretary general to oversee daily management and implement resolutions; a steering committee, appointed by the directors; and several subcommittees, which any members could attend. These committees would act as forums, draw up recommendations, and carry out much of the association's work. To ensure fast decision making, the board was authorized to approve motions through a simple majority vote. The annual general assembly could also approve resolutions by a simple majority.

Some members of the GPCA's founding board gather with secretary general Abdullah Al-Hagbani for a photo in 2006. *From left to right:* Al-Hagbani, Abdulrahman Jawahery, Mohamed Al-Mady, Sa'ad Al-Shuwaib, Hamad Al-Terkait, and Hubert Puchner.

On that first day, the board appointed its chairman, vice chairman, and treasurer—Mohamed Al-Mady of SABIC, Hamad Al-Terkait of EQUATE, and Hubert Puchner of Borouge, respectively. It decided on a budget for 2006, set membership fees, appointed a secretary general (Abdullah Al-Hagbani, SABIC's Dubai Office head), and fixed a date for the next meeting.

All that remained was for Al-Mady to meet with reporters. He gave a short speech, outlining how the GPCA would work in such areas as environmental protection, safety and regulation, logistics, training, and the promotion of downstream industry. He pointed out that the establishment of the GPCA was "a first step in creating a global presence for the regional petrochemical and chemical industry." The GPCA would act as an industry spokesperson; it would promote cooperation between members and related bodies both inside and outside the Arabian Gulf region, organize conferences, and encourage scientific research. Overall, it would identify, advance, and manage common interests.

Anticipating concerns that the GPCA might function as a cartel, Al-Hagbani was quick to spread the message that anything to do with production policy, reference mechanisms, or pricing was simply not on the agenda. He stressed that the GPCA was not a cartel and would not allow collusion to take place.

Great Expectations

Other board members expressed similar thoughts. Hamad Al Nuaimi, then general manager at QVC, called for "close cooperation and exchange of information, especially on such issues as safety, environment, and sustainable development, as well as training and maintenance." Hamad Al-Mohannadi, then general manager of QAPCO, wanted the GPCA to "encourage research related to the industry and provide solutions on scientific and technical issues, promote the development of human resources within the industry, and organize industrial conferences and seminars." Abdulrahman Jawahery, then general manager at GPIC, wanted the GPCA to include consumers and other supporting services, such as financial institutions, technology providers, research facilities, and service providers, to achieve efficient industrial integration across the region. The GPCA could play a role in helping its members expand regional logistics facilities and adhere to environmental legislation.

The GPCA's treasurer, Hubert Puchner, spoke of promoting free and fair trade and competition and providing development support for industry. "The association will focus on plastics, and promote plastic products by encouraging industry innovation and improving the industry's image," he told a reporter. Members would "reap the benefits of an increasingly collaborative approach" as the association matured. Environmental issues would be high on the agenda:

> We will try to educate communities and municipalities about plastics and environmental issues associated with plastics, give them support, and explain the importance of the contribution that plastics make to society.

Industry consultant Roger Green of Nexant ChemSystems saw the GPCA's creation as a coming of age for the region in global terms, enabling manufacturers to present a common view. Some were more cautious. Ed James of the *Middle East Economic Digest* wrote in November 2006,

> The regional petrochemicals industry has long been fragmented and disjointed, so it can only be a good thing that companies work together to reach a common goal through the GPCA. Although there will inevitably be some accusations of monopolistic practices, if the sector is to mature in the Gulf, it will need a body that can help regulate and speak on its behalf. It will now be up to its members to determine whether it becomes a mere talking shop or a real force for change.

Al-Mady's aim was for the GPCA to establish "global engagement," working with similar organizations in Europe, Latin America, the United States, and Asia. The challenge was "to stay proactive, especially with regard to the environment and regulatory controls."

Open for Business

That June, Al-Hagbani, acting as the GPCA's new secretary general, told the MEED Petrochemicals Conference that invitations to join the GPCA would soon be sent out. "Any company involved in the sector can join. It's an excellent networking opportunity; members can exchange opinions, share knowledge and experience, and advocate the growth, development, and prosperity of the industry in the Arabian Gulf."

On 1 July 2006, the GPCA opened its first headquarters on Sheikh Zayed Road in Dubai. Daily operations were overseen by Al-Hagbani. By September, he had a team of three to look after administration and finance, promotions, membership and events, and working committees. "We started gearing up for our crucial role right from the word go." The office began to hum.

Ribbon-cutting ceremony at the opening of the first GPCA office. *From left to right:* Abdullah Al-Hagbani, Abdulrahman Jawahery, Mohamed Al-Mady, Sa'ad Al-Shuwaib, Hamad Al-Terkait, and Hubert Puchner.

Dubai had always been the logical, long-anticipated location for GPCA headquarters. Its economy combined tourism, banking, and other service industries, and it was endowed with excellent infrastructure and transportation links. Al-Terkait called it "a good neutral base for all of us." Thanks to its open economic policy, minimal governmental control, low crime rate, political stability, and geographical location at the heart of fast-growing markets, Dubai was rapidly becoming a cosmopolitan, global hub. Moreover, it was an easy place to get things done. As Mohamed Al-Azdi noted, "Dubai has the least red tape in the Arabian Gulf."

The GPCA's office became the main administrative center for the association as it built its membership ranks and developed common positions on industry issues. Very soon there was a "burgeoning list of companies wishing to become members or affiliates" and desiring access to networking opportunities.

First Steps

By November 2006, the GPCA had signed up thirty members, including top-tier international firms, such as ExxonMobil Chemical, Royal Dutch/Shell Group, Dow Chemical Company, and Borealis. Twenty more members would quickly follow. In the first flush of success, ambitions expanded: soon the aim was to exceed the hundred members' threshold.

"Essentially we are three things," explained Al-Hagbani in an in-depth interview: 1) a spokesperson for the petrochemicals industry in the region; 2) "the ultimate and undisputed reference point" for information and data about the regional industry; and 3) "a platform for change."

The GPCA wanted to play "a proactive role in becoming a credible source of industry information not available elsewhere." Serving as a reference point was a way to represent common interests and could be achieved by building a reliable data bank of production information.

Saudi Chevron Phillips in Jubail.

By the end of 2006, the GPCA had already started to identify and understand production levels and capacities in the region. The association would require regional members to provide data each year to increase transparency for planning. The data would be used to create an annual report to furnish trustworthy information to the member companies.

Objectives, Accomplishments, Plans

For the small GPCA staff, the immediate objectives were to set up infrastructure, expand the membership base, develop and build committees, recognize and address common issues, and put together a world-class annual event ("a forum") for the industry.

By the end of 2006, the team had launched a website ("a treasure trove of information") and was moving toward the quarterly publication of *Gulf Chemical Insight*—or *Insight*—to advocate for development in petrochemical and chemical industries. Writing in the first annual report, Al-Mady described how the GPCA had already "grown into a strong, vibrant association" and "taken center stage."

The Arabian Gulf region was growing rapidly in status as a global hub for the chemical production, and the GPCA was "proud to be playing a pivotal role in promoting cooperation, understanding, and information sharing" for that region. Listening, learning, and engaging would be key to long-term success in this

Through our Middle East joint ventures, Chevron Phillips Chemical Company LLC has been a long-standing member and supporter of the GPCA. We strongly believe in the GPCA's mission to support the growth and sustainable development of the vibrant petrochemical and chemical industries in the Gulf region. Our core values of safety, sustainability, and corporate transparency align with GPCA's mission, specifically, its advocacy of Responsible Care, the chemical industry's initiative to improve health, safety, and environmental performance. We're proud of our involvement in the GPCA through our joint ventures and look forward to continued participation in this valuable organization.

—Peter Cella, president and CEO, Chevron Phillips Chemical Company

new era of cooperation, while continuing dialogue would help the industry reach opinion leaders at large.

As Al-Hagbani summed up in his report at the end of 2006, the GPCA was "a much-needed" body established at "the most opportune time" as a "major step" for the regional industry, which was reinforcing its position as a global manufacturing center for basic petrochemicals.

3 Developing Capacity, Expanding Benefits, Growing Membership

By the end of 2006, GPCA membership had grown to more than sixty companies—a testimony to the enthusiasm with which the organization was greeted, to its success in representing the interests of its members, and to the dedication of its staff.

At the outset, learning and networking were the main benefits of membership in the GPCA. The association's leadership focused the organization on creating networking-learning platforms that provided the opportunity to connect with industry people from inside and outside the Arabian Gulf region to share knowledge and to exchange perspectives.

One of the most important functions of the association was to serve as a much-needed networking platform in a highly competitive global business. Through its Annual Forum (see Chapter 5) and eventually through a range of events, such as summits, conferences, and workshops, the GPCA offered a venue where people from the Gulf region and beyond could come together and get to know each other, setting the stage for collaboration and mutual assistance. These networking and learning opportunities were directed by GPCA committees (see Chapter 4) made up of representatives of member companies. The work of the committees was supported by the staff of the GPCA.

Expanding Headquarters

In November 2007, since the GPCA was already outgrowing its physical home, the board aired the idea of a move to new headquarters. Directors raised the matter again in March 2008 because there were space constraints and the association was in an expansion mode. They made the decision to recruit more staff. They added a committee coordinator, two meeting coordinators, and a coordinator for an initiative on Responsible Care. That June, the possibility of relocating to Abu Dhabi or Bahrain was on the table, and an independent adviser was engaged to assess the pros and cons of each of the proposed cities. Based on the recommendations, the Board of Directors concluded in October 2008 that the advantages of the Dubai location—friendly regulations for nonprofits, a great service sector,

Ribbon cutting at the opening of the Aspect Tower office. *From left to right*: Hamad Al-Terkait, Mohamed Al-Mady, and Abdulwahab Al-Sadoun.

and so forth—outweighed any disadvantages. The search began for a fresh home in Dubai.

With regard to that, the first step for the board was to decide whether it should lease or purchase the new headquarters. After some discussion, it concluded that it would be wiser to buy, and the secretary general was authorized to focus on purchasing GPCA's new home. In December 2010, the GPCA moved from the modest two-room office, which had served as headquarters since 2006, into a 3,400-square-foot office located in Aspect Towers, Business Bay, in Dubai. That location would serve the GPCA well for nearly five years, but in 2015, the GPCA would move again—this time into a 10,500-square-foot office located in the landmark Vision Tower in the Business Bay district, which was inaugurated on 15 March 2015.

A New Secretary General

In April 2009, Abdullah Al-Hagbani stepped down from his role as secretary general at the GPCA, and the position was filled by Abdulwahab Al-Sadoun.

Al-Sadoun came to the GPCA with a deep understanding of the petrochemical industry in the Arabian Gulf and its future perspectives, gained from his broad professional experience, including his work with the Gulf Organization for Industrial Consulting in Qatar, which had also played a role in paving the way for the GPCA's formation.

In his first message to the GPCA's members, Al-Sadoun underlined the organization's central role of fostering cooperation not only among its members but more broadly in the global chemical community. His message and vision were inspiring:

> It is my opinion that the issues facing our industries are too important for us to tackle in isolation, and the challenges and opportunities that confront our companies are too large to consider taking them on single-handedly. In today's increasingly competitive environment, "sustained cooperation" is the key to a more

promising future for our industry: a future in which the chemicals and petrochemicals produced in the Gulf region help millions of people to realize the promise of a better standard of living and greater prosperity.

Increasing Benefits, Adding Value

Within months of becoming secretary general, Al-Sadoun unveiled a road map to the board that outlined ways to raise revenue, improve the effectiveness of the working committees, increase the GPCA's visibility and its advocacy role, and expand its capacity to deliver "knowledge-based content." The main points of Al-Sadoun's proposal presented to the board on June 2009 were as follows:

1. Increasing the Revenue Stream

Annual revenue could be increased by raising the cash flow from networking events. He sought to have a 30:70 ratio of membership dues to non-dues revenue.

2. Structural Changes with Committees

Emphasizing that the GPCA operational model would be centered on "working for members through members," Al-Sadoun stressed the need to introduce structural changes to the committees, as well as selecting more senior executives empowered by the companies' management to sit on the committees. Committee work was to be made more useful by eliminating the Steering Committee, which had proved less than effective. Henceforth, a manager of committees and global affairs (a newly created staff position) was to coordinate the working committees, the priorities of which were to be set by the Executive Committee of the Board, which Al-Sadoun also proposed to increase by one member. In addition, Al-Sadoun advised that two new committees be created: a Fertilizer Committee and an Advocacy Committee. To provide more focus with higher accountability to the committees, Al-Sadoun suggested having each of the six committees chaired by a member of the board. This proposal was endorsed unanimously and reflected on the performance and accomplishments of the committees.

3. Improved Visibility and the Ability to Serve as Advocate

Al-Sadoun contended that the GPCA's long-term success required a multistage marketing and communication plan, one element of which was to carry out a range of activities that would improve the profile of the organization regionally and globally. This included such actions as the adoption of Responsible Care, the creation of awards, active participation in events inside and outside of the region, and sponsorship of publications of broad interest that showed the socioeconomic impact of the industry on the region.

4. Knowledge-Based Content

The GPCA had taken some steps to provide its members with information that would help them in decision making and planning. Al-Sadoun called for a much bigger effort in this area in an attempt to provide value. He foresaw the regular publication of reliable, professionally developed reports, surveys, and forecasts that would serve not only members but also the global chemical industry.

Membership Growth and Development

The GPCA has always offered two membership categories: full membership and associate membership. The former is available to chemical enterprises with production facilities within the Arabian Gulf region producing more than one hundred kilotons annually. Only full members are eligible to nominate members to the board.

In 2006, associate membership was available to a range of entities and individuals:

- Arabian Gulf chemical enterprises producing less than one hundred kilotons annually;

- Chemical producers from outside the Arabian Gulf region regardless of the volume of their annual production;

- Companies from both the region and outside the region that provide chemical producers with such services as shipping, engineering, and marketing;

- Companies and organizations that are directly involved in chemical and petrochemical trade and industry; and

- Companies, organizations, and individuals not fitting any of the categories noted above, which were assigned the category "other professionals."

In June 2007, the Board of Directors concluded that despite the increases in membership to 28 full members and 60 associate members, still more efforts were needed. The directors set the ambitious goal of 160 members by the end of the year. At the same time, the board decided to establish new revenue streams to reduce the organization's dependence on membership dues. By the end of 2008, membership reached 144. In 2009, however, in the throes of the global Great Recession, membership dropped to 135, with 99 in the Arabian Gulf, 16 in Europe, 12 in Asia, 7 in the Americas, and one in Africa. The United Arab Emirates (UAE) and Saudi Arabia together were home base for 80 members. Qatar had 8; Kuwait, 6; Bahrain, 5; and Oman, 3.

In 2009, as part of his vision for the GPCA, Al-Sadoun proposed changes to the membership structure. Before June 2009, new members had been required to pay both an initiation fee and annual membership dues, with full members paying an initiation fee of $25,000 and associate member chemical companies paying an initiation fee of $10,000. Al-Sadoun suggested eliminating initiation fees, arguing that this would encourage companies to join the GPCA and, more particularly, would increase the number of full members. Expanded membership, he contended, would establish a stable larger cash flow to the association. He also suggested eliminating the category of "other professional." In support of these proposed changes, he noted that such organizations as the EPCA and the National Petrochemical and Refiners Association (today known as the AFPM [American Fuel

The GPCA was an initiative by many of our colleagues who realized the importance of improving communications among the main participants in the emerging petrochemicals and chemicals industry in the Gulf. It is my humble opinion that none of us who participated in the establishment of the GPCA had expected the emergence of the organization to be such a powerful communications platform for our industry in the Gulf and globally. The great strength of the GPCA is the harmony among its founders and members, which puts cooperation ahead of confrontation and establishment of consensus ahead of forcing personal views; all these attributes are at the core of GPCA strengths.

Since inception the GPCA has played the important role of providing communications platforms for the regional companies to address vital issues for the industry, society, and environment. The GPCA has also facilitated global dialogue between the industry players in the region and internationally: if you look at the diversity of the speakers and attendees of the Annual Forum, it gives clear indication of that. I am completely optimistic that the GPCA—with the growth of experience of its general secretariat, the growing global importance of its members, and the full commitment of its Board of Directors to its further growth and sophistication in tackling the future challenges of our industry—will continue to grow in importance regionally and globally.

—*Moayyed Al-Qurtas, former CEO of Tasnee*

and Petrochemical Manufacturers]) handled membership in a similar fashion. These changes were accepted by the GPCA's board.

Before 2009, SABIC and five of its subsidiaries were among the full members. To ensure that all SABIC's regional affiliates benefited from the membership privileges, Al-Sadoun proposed to the board in 2011 the introduction of the "corporate membership" within the full member category. The new corporate membership would apply to conglomerates and to groups of subsidiaries in which a parent company has an equity share of 50 percent or more. The board endorsed the proposal, and after receiving approval from the 2012 General Assembly, the membership categories became the following:

Full Members
Corporate Members

Individual Members

Associate Members
Small GCC Producers

International Producers (Non–Arabian Gulf)

Service Companies

Business Partners

Al-Sadoun's proposal regarding membership structure worked hand in hand with his suggestions about enhancing the GPCA's advocacy and educational role and the effectiveness of its committees to expand membership. In 2010, as the Great Recession stabilized and began to retreat, membership rose once again, and the GPCA finally reached its goal of 160 members, of whom 36 were full members (Figure 1).

FIGURE 1. Growth of GPCA Membership, 2006–2014

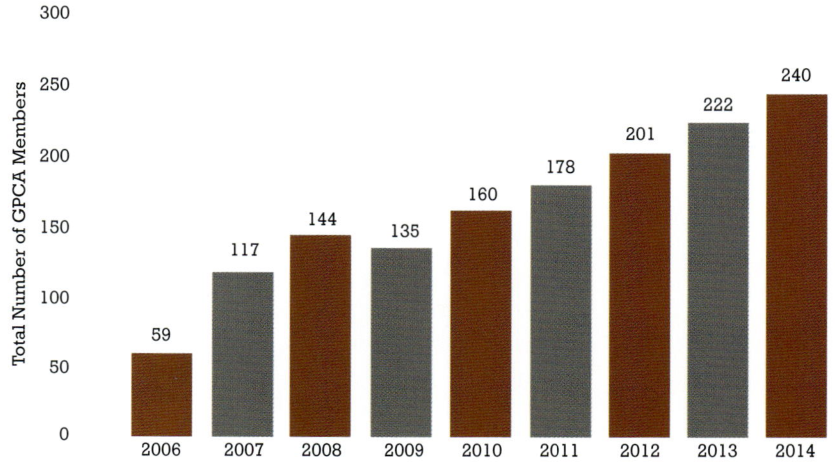

With an improving economy, membership grew steadily over the next few years, passing the two hundred mark by 2012. Importantly, it was evident that the GPCA was attracting the most significant companies of its home region. By 2013, GPCA members were responsible for 95 percent of the Arabian Gulf region's total petrochemical output.

Increased membership also reflected the growing global role the Gulf industry was poised to play. In 2011, Al-Sadoun declared,

> Our platform has grown in stature with each year of our relatively short existence. This is due, in large measure, to the commitment, the high level of interest, and the faith that our members have reposed in our charter.

High levels of participation highlighted how the association's leadership enjoyed the confidence of its members and how it had made excellent progress in a short span of time. Increased membership also reflected the strongly growing interest of the global petrochemical and chemical industry in the Gulf region, and in the important role its industry was beginning to assume.

Hamad Al-Terkait saw the association's success as a reflection of the region's great need for such an organization:

> The Arabian Gulf's seat at the table of the global trade associations was empty for many, many years. There were no Gulf representatives because companies from our region were not connected to any one association. Each company spoke as an individual. Now we have one organization that represents the Gulf, which itself now constitutes a significant percentage of the global volume of petrochemicals.

> People have recognized the value of having this association. When the members of the GPCA saw there was a real benefit, they put in all their effort to make the GPCA very successful. We have started late, but it's never too late. The success we're having today is compensating us for the years of not having a voice.

The eight petrochemical majors who had founded the association in 2006 had "a grand vision but initially modest targets and expectations." In time, the GPCA would "tick the boxes" to become "a key cornerstone in a global context, promoting the interests of the region's top chemical and petrochemical producers like never before."

In 2014, the GPCA's membership was 240, with 34 full members. The membership's geographic range was impressive, with over one-third being companies from outside the Gulf. The GPCA had become a regional organization that addressed issues of interest to the global petrochemical industry, reflected in the steady increase in GPCA members from outside of the region. In 2007, such members constituted 24 percent of membership, and today they constitute 31 percent (Table 1).

Table 1. Membership by Member Location, 2007 and 2014

Region	2007		2014	
	Total Number	**Percentage of Total**	**Total Number**	**Percentage of Total**
Middle East	58	76.3	166	69.20
Asia	11	14.5	20	8.30
Europe	4	5.2	33	13.75
North America	2	2.6	17	7.00
Africa	1	1.3	4	1.60

Al-Sadoun's efforts to expand the sources of the GPCA's revenue stream have been successful. During the GPCA's startup years, membership fees composed the majority of the organization's income. In 2006, membership fees composed about 79 percent of its income. As the GPCA increasingly began offering well-attended and highly regarded events, the percentage dropped. In 2014, membership fees were the source of only 22.9 percent of the GPCA income.

To better understand the effectiveness of the various services provided to members, the GPCA secretariat conducted three membership satisfaction surveys: in 2007, 2010, and 2014.

The aim of these surveys was twofold: to gauge the performance of the GPCA in providing services and to gather the opinions of industry leaders, members, and nonmembers regarding different activities and programs launched by the GPCA. The results not only helped identify the GPCA's strengths and weaknesses, but they also pointed to opportunities to expand and enhance services. The latest survey was executed by Edelman, a public relations firm, and enjoyed a high level of participation, with 167 members, 6 former members, and 15 industry leaders responding.

Further, since 2009, the GPCA has steadily expanded benefits to members. First, it has increasingly served as a source of information through commissioned reports on key topics and also through access to an online database. These services have helped members make business decisions and set out company strategy. Second, it has taken on the role of advocate for the Arabian Gulf petrochemical industry, manifested, for example, in efforts to improve the public perception of plastics and in addressing antisubsidies cases initiated in the European Union and antidumping measures taken by India and China vis-à-vis producers in Saudi Arabia and Oman. This expansion of the GPCA's role has been paralleled by a greater professionalization of the association, reflected in a professional staff possessing a range of expertise.

The Board

In 2009, the GPCA elected to keep its current chairman and vice chairman, Mohamed Al-Mady and Hamad Al-Terkait, through the administrative transition. The association also had an executive committee, composed of the board

Delegates gather at the third GPCA Annual Forum.

chair, vice chair, treasurer (Abdulaziz Alhajri, CEO of Borouge), and one additional board member (Hamad Al Nuaimi, CEO of QVC), whose role was to submit strategic and major positioning issues to the board for decisions. Committee members were elected every three years.

Plans to expand the board itself also came to fruition; the number of directors grew from eight to fifteen. Wanting to make itself "even more representative of the regional industry," the GPCA elected to its board key executives of seven leading Gulf chemical companies: Mohamed Al-Azdi of ChemaWEyaat; Ahmad Al-Ohali of Sipchem (Saudi International Petrochemical Company); Marwan

The GPCA has so rapidly evolved due to the foresight and ambition of its leaders. It has been clear for many years that the Middle East would be an important force in the chemicals industry. What many people did not fully recognize, however, was the regional resolve to become as powerful a force in the chemicals space as it has been historically in the energy space. It has been my personal pleasure to have participated in five major projects in various countries that have helped make this a reality.

—*James Gallogly, former CEO of LyondellBasell*

Nusair of Alujain; Ziad Al-Labban of Petro Rabigh; Khalifa Al Sowaidi of the Qatar Fertilizer Company (QAFCO); Ali Hassan Al-Sidiky of Qatar Petroleum; and an empty seat was kept for Oman. The eight GPCA founders were also given permanent seats on the board. Al-Terkait recalls,

> We said, "We need to expand the board. There are hundreds of chemical companies. Let's find a solution by saying that any company which produces more than a hundred thousand tons a year can be a member and can have a board seat. We don't want any single company to monopolize this platform." To sit at one table and talk about common issues was not easy. But we gathered fifteen board members, all CEOs of manufacturing companies, all at one table to talk about common issues.

In 2010, the association added three additional staff members and established a communication advisory board to supersede its communications and promotions committee. The website, a critical component of the GPCA, was overhauled and updated. Al-Sadoun, the secretary general, described the website:

> It is an ideal way to reach out to professionals and engage them in our global network. At the touch of a button, we can provide real-time information, interact directly with professionals, and bring people together to connect, share, and access valuable resources. Our aim is to help them succeed.

By 2013, the GPCA had come a long way from its modest beginnings, as was apparent from the important benefits it offered to its members. Examples of these advantages included help in implementing the Responsible Care program and the opportunity to reach a global audience through the GPCA's website, quarterly newsletter, and annual membership directory.

Over the past ten years, the members of the GPCA Boards of Directors were instrumental to the success of the organization (see Table 2).

Table 2. Members of the GPCA's Boards of Directors (2006–2015)

First Board Members (2006–2009)

Mohamed Al-Mady (Vice Chairman and CEO, SABIC) – Board Chairman

Hamad Al-Terkait (President and CEO, EQUATE) – Vice Chairman

Hubert Puchner (CEO, Borouge) – Treasurer

Mohamed Al-Azdi (CEO, ChemaWEyaat)

Hamad Al-Mohannadi (Vice Chairman and General Manager, QAPCO)

Moayyed Al-Qurtas (CEO, Tasnee)

Sa'ad Al-Shuwaib (Chairman and Managing Director, PIC)

Abdulrahman Jawahery (General Manager, GPIC)

Second Board Members (2009–2012)

Mohamed Al-Mady (Vice Chairman and CEO, SABIC) – Board Chairman

Hamad Al-Terkait (President and CEO, EQUATE) – Vice Chairman

Abdulaziz Alhajri (CEO, Borouge) – Treasurer

Mohammed Al-Azdi (CEO, ChemaWEyaat)

Hamed Al Dhahab (CEO, Oman PolyPropylene LLC)

Ziad Al-Labban (President and CEO, PetroRabigh)

Mohammed Al Mulla (Vice Chairman and CEO, QAPCO)

Hamad Rashed Al Nuaimi (CEO, QVC)

Ahmad Al-Ohali (CEO, Sipchem)

Moayyed Al-Qurtas (Vice Chairman and CEO, Tasnee)

Ali Hassan Al-Sidiky (Director, Qatar Petroleum),

Khalifa Al Sowaidi (Vice Chairman and CEO, QAFCO)

Maha Mulla Hussain (Chairman and Managing Director, PIC)

Abdulrahman Jawahery (President, GPIC)

Marwan N. Nusair (President and CEO, Alujain Corporation)

Third Board Members (2012–2015)

Mohamed Al-Mady (Vice Chairman and CEO, SABIC) – Board Chairman

Rashed Al Shamsi (Petrochemicals Director, ADNOC) – Vice Chairman

Abdulaziz Alhajri (CEO, Borouge) – Treasurer

Mohammed Al-Azdi (CEO, ChemaWEyaat)

Musab Al Mahrouqi (CEO, Orpic)

Mohammed Al Mulla (Vice Chairman and CEO, QAPCO)

Hamad Rashed Al Nuaimi (CEO, QVC)

Ahmad Al-Ohali (CEO, Sipchem)

Moayyed Al-Qurtas (Vice Chairman and CEO, Tasnee)

Khalifa Al Sowaidi (Vice Chairman and CEO, QAFCO)

Abdullah Al-Suwailem (President and CEO, PetroRabigh)

Maha Mulla Hussain (Chairman and Managing Director, PIC)

Mohammad Husain (President and CEO, EQUATE)

Abdulrahman Jawahery (President, GPIC)

Abdulaziz Judaimi (Vice President, Saudi Aramco)

Fourth Board Members (2015–2017)

Rashed Al Shamsi (Petrochemicals Director, ADNOC) – Board Chairman

Yousef Al Benyan (Vice Chairman and CEO, SABIC) – Vice Chairman

Abdulaziz Alhajri (CEO, Borouge) – Treasurer

Hamad Rashed Al Nuaimi (CEO, QVC) – Member of Executive Committee

Ahmed Al Meheri (CEO, ChemaWEyaat)

Musab Al Mahrouqi (CEO, Orpic)

Mohammed Al Mulla (Vice Chairman and CEO, QAPCO)

Ahmad Al-Ohali (CEO, Sipchem)

Mutlaq Al-Morieshed (Vice Chairman and CEO, Tasnee)

Khalifa Al Sowaidi (Vice Chairman and CEO, QAFCO)

Muhammed Al-Hajiri (GM, QP)

Asaad Al Saad (Chairman and Managing Director, PIC)

Mohammad Husain (President and CEO, EQUATE)

Abdulrahman Jawahery (President, GPIC)

Warren Wilder (Chemicals Vice President, Saudi Aramco)

Board of Directors 1 and Steering Committee members, 2006–2009.

Back: Homood Al-Tuwaijri,vice president for corporate control, SABIC (Steering Committee); Abdul Rahman Al-Abdullah, marketing manager, QAPCO (Steering Committee); Moayyed Al-Qurtas, vice chairman and CEO, Tasnee; Yusuf Ebrahim Fakhroo, administration manager, GPIC (Steering Committee); Mohamed Al-Azdi, CEO, ChemaWEyaat; Jamal Algharabally, marketing manager, PIC; Saleh Al-Alweet, SABIC; Abdel Al-Munifi, business director, EQUATE (Steering Committee); Walid Al-Hammad, general manager, Tasnee.

Front: Abdullah Al-Hagbani, secretary general, GPCA; Hubert Puchner, CEO, Borouge; Hamad Al-Terkait, president and CEO, EQUATE; Mohamed Al-Mady, vice chairman and CEO, SABIC; Sa'ad Al-Shuwaib, chairman and managing director, PIC; Abdulrahman Jawahery, general manager, GPIC; Hamad Al-Mohannadi, vice chairman and general manager, QAPCO.

Board of Directors 2, 2009–2012.

Back: Abdulrahman Jawahery, president, GPIC; Ahmad Al-Ohali, CEO, Sipchem; Hamad Al Nuaimi, CEO, QVC; Ali Hassan Al-Sidiky, director, Qatar Petroleum; Mohammed Al Mulla, vice chairman and CEO, QAPCO; Marwan N. Nusair, president and CEO, Alujain Corporation; Ziad Al-Labban, president and CEO, PetroRabigh; Hamed Al Dhahab, CEO, Oman PolyPropylene LLC.

Front: Mohamed Al-Azdi, CEO, ChemaWEyaat; Khalifa Al Sowaidi, vice chairman and CEO, QAFCO; Hamad Al-Terkait, president and CEO, EQUATE; Mohamed Al-Mady, vice chairman and CEO, SABIC; Abdulaziz Alhajri, CEO, Borouge; Maha Mulla Hussain, chairman and managing director, PIC; Moayyed Al-Qurtas, vice chairman and CEO, Tasnee.

Board of Directors 3, 2012–2015.

Back: Abdullah Al-Suwailem, president and CEO, PetroRabigh; Abdulaziz Judaimi, vice president, Saudi Aramco; Hamad Al Nuaimi, CEO, QVC; Ahmad Al-Ohali, CEO, Sipchem; Abdulaziz Alhajri, CEO, Borouge; Khalifa Al Sowaidi, vice chairman and CEO, QAFCO; Mohammad Husain, president and CEO, EQUATE; Abdulrahman Jawahery, president, GPIC.

Front: Musab Al Mahrouqi, CEO, Orpic; Maha Mulla Hussain, chairman and managing director, PIC; Rashed Al Shamsi, petrochemicals director, ADNOC; Mohamed Al-Mady, vice chairman and CEO, SABIC; Mohamed Al-Azdi, CEO, ChemaWEyaat; Moayyed Al-Qurtas, vice chairman and CEO, Tasnee.

Missing: Mohammed Al Mulla, vice chairman and CEO, QAPCO.

Board of Directors 4, 2015–2017.

Back: Warren Wilder, vice president, chemicals, Saudi Aramco; Ahmed Al Mheiri, CEO, ChemaWEyaat; Musab Al Mahrouqi, CEO, Orpic; Ahmad Al-Ohali, CEO, Sipchem; Khalifa Al Sowaidi, vice chairman and CEO, QAFCO; Mohammed Al Mulla, vice chairman and CEO, QAPCO.

Front: Mutlaq Al-Morished, CEO, Tasnee; Hamad Al Nuaimi, CEO, QVC; Rashed Al Shamsi, petrochemicals director, ADNOC; Yousif Al-Benyan, vice chairman and CEO, SABIC; Abdulaziz Alhajri, CEO, Borouge; Mohammed Al-Hajri, vice president, Downstream Development, Qatar Petroleum; Mohammad Husain, president and CEO, EQUATE.

Missing: Abdulrahman Jawahery, president, GPIC.

4 Working Communities

Setup and Strategy

One founding aim of the GPCA was to promote cooperation in a range of areas. To facilitate this, three committees were formed at the outset: Human Resources; Safety, Health, and the Environment; and Communication and Promotion. The work of the committees was supported by the GPCA's staff, which organized seminars and workshops that would bring member companies in contact not only with each other but also with experts from outside the region.

The GPCA was keen to play an active role as a platform for knowledge sharing and best practices exchange. In June 2007, the association held its first workshop, dealing with performance management as conducted by a U.S. company, Personnel Decisions International. Two additional workshops quickly followed: one in October dealt with REACH (Registration, Evaluation, and Authorization of Chemicals) and antitrust; a second, in November, dealt with contractor safety.

Delegate numbers were low—no more than thirty people attended each workshop—but interest was rising. Having pledged to be "proactive," the GPCA also set up a process to identify issues important to the region. This process revealed that corporate social responsibility was a significant issue for members and so was taken up for immediate action.

The GPCA Safety, Health, and Environment (SHE) Committee was launched on 10 May 2007. It quickly identified CO_2 emissions, process safety management, and Responsible Care as focus areas. The implementation of Responsible Care by the GPCA board was seen as especially important, and in December 2009, the board unanimously endorsed the implementation of Responsible Care in the Arabian Gulf States. The board also endorsed the suggestion of the secretariat that the SHE Committee be renamed the Responsible Care Committee. The GPCA's success in bringing about the adoption of Responsible Care would make it part of an international cooperative effort by the chemical community to improve health, safety, and environmental performance. It would also lead in a few years to the GPCA's full membership in the International Council for Chemical Associations (ICCA).

> ***Responsible Care***
>
> Responsible Care is the chemical industry's comprehensive health, safety, security, and environmental (HSSE) performance improvement initiative. It was conceived in 1984 by the Canadian Chemical Producers Association. Global acceptance was signaled by the International Council of Chemical Association's launch of the Responsible Care Global Charter in 2006 at the U.N.-led International Conference on Chemicals Management in Dubai.
>
> A Responsible Care Management System (RCMS) yields many important business benefits. Implementation focuses on improving performance in HSSE through lower emissions, less waste, fewer injuries, and more secure facilities and operations. An RCMS can lead to lower operating costs through more efficient and reliable use of labor and energy, meaning less money is spent on handling waste and emissions, and less time is spent dealing with the distractions of incidents or compliance problems.

In 2006, the GPCA member Borouge was the first company in the Gulf region to sign up for the Responsible Care Global Charter. Borouge consultant Andre Crous quickly followed up with a presentation to the GPCA's Board of Directors on how to implement a Responsible Care program.

In October 2007, the GPCA made a presentation to the Responsible Care Leadership Group in Paris about efforts to bring Responsible Care to the Arabian Gulf region. Borouge's CEO Abdulaziz Alhajri spoke of his hope that the GPCA would be successful in its efforts to join the Responsible Care program and said that it was committed to the charter.

GPCA chairman Mohamed Al-Mady noted,

> Keeping the environment clean and following strict safety procedures are essential for good business practices. In view of this, the GPCA is striving to get the message of safety and concern for the environment to all chemical companies in the region and to their partners. The association's Safety, Health, and Environment Committee is reviewing the possibility of joining the Responsible Care program run by the ICCA. A protocol for sharing best practices and incident data is also being worked on.

Al-Mady and Al-Terkait were agreed that the GPCA should apply a "top-down" approach to Responsible Care. The committee would work toward implementing Responsible Care, and the initiative would become a key strategic driver for the association's activities. "We believe our region has much to gain from pursuing this initiative," said Al-Sadoun.

In his turn, in November 2008, Al-Mady told *Chemical Week*,

The GPCA has a role in stressing the importance of corporate social responsibility among our member companies. As major companies in the region, we must be good corporate citizens in the geographic areas in which we operate. We must provide an environment in which our workforce can operate safely and productively, while developing as valued employees and as people. And, of course, we must be respectful and caring toward our environment.

As an important industry, which utilizes hydrocarbons as its main feedstock, we must dig deeper into understanding and evaluating the issue of global warming and various proposed solutions such as a global carbon-tracing regime. We must evaluate the impact of proposed carbon reduction schemes on our industry and how we will manage our business if such changes evolve.

On 12 November 2008, the GPCA invited Responsible Care specialists to present the initiative to association members at a panel event in Dubai; it hired two consultants to help implement the initiative, and it invited its members to send representatives to the Responsible Care working group that had been set up by the SHE Committee. A key milestone in the implementation of the Responsible Care journey occurred in 2009, when the GPCA board unanimously endorsed implementation of the Responsible Care program in the GCC region, renamed the SHE Committee as the Responsible Care Committee, and appointed board member Abdulrahman Jawahery as its chairman.

In 2009, this committee organized seminars on such topics as fugitive emissions, mechanical integrity, management of change, and Responsible Care; it also wrote articles and attended such events as the Responsible Care Leadership Group meeting in Moscow. During this period, the committee was chaired by Yasir Abdulrahim of GPIC, who steered the committee toward the implementation of the Responsible Care Program in the Arabian Gulf. The implementation drive gained momentum with the appointment of Tahir Jamal Qadir—a veteran industry health, safety, and environment expert—to lead the program in early 2010. Qadir was assigned to that role by SabTank, a subsidiary of SABIC, till March 2014. In 2011, the Responsible Care Committee elected Alan Izzard, Borouge's corporate vice chair for environmental health and safety, to succeed Abdulrahim.

Tahir Jamal Qadir addressing a Responsible Care Workshop.

Alan Izzard, GPCA's current director of Responsible Care.

The Responsible Care Committee was a key player in securing the commitment of member companies to put Responsible Care into practice. In early 2010, the GPCA developed an implementation plan with clear milestones and timelines, beginning with the CEOs of the full members signing a declaration of support to apply the Responsible Care seven management codes. This was followed by the GPCA taking steps to register the Responsible Care logo tagline (Our Commitment to Sustainability) in both English and Arabic within the six GCC states and issued usage criteria.

By the end of 2011, over 80 percent of the GPCA's membership had signed the Declaration of Support for Responsible Care, completed self-assessments, and adopted the use of the Responsible Care logo. In 2012, the GPCA prepared and issued four more codes of management practice for Responsible Care. In 2013, the GPCA published its first Performance Metrics Report, which highlighted the performance of the Responsible Care signatories for the period 2010 to 2012.

During the GPCA fifth Annual Forum held on 7–9 December 2010, the GPCA Responsible Care Program was given a boost by signing a memorandum of understanding, with the American Chemistry Council (ACC) serving as the GPCA's mentor. The memorandum was signed by the chairmen of the two associations, Mohamed Al-Mady and Steven Pryor, president of ExxonMobil Chemicals. The GPCA presented the aim "to champion the Responsible Care initiative among members" as one of its main strategic objectives. It hoped to develop and install Responsible Care systems and to earn ICCA recognition by the end of 2010.

The Passage to Full ICCA Membership

As evidence of its commitment to the Responsible Care Global Program, the GPCA offered to host the annual meeting of the Responsible Care Leadership Group of ICCA. This invitation was accepted, and in September 2010, representatives from fifty countries gathered in Dubai to discuss Responsible Care and to review GPCA's Responsible Care program. The gathering unanimously endorsed GPCA's application for full membership in ICCA, thus paving the way for a fast-track implementation of Responsible Care in the Arabian Gulf and qualifying the GPCA to become a full member of ICCA.

The ICCA Responsible
Care Leadership Group
that met in Dubai.

In December 2010, the GPCA applied for ICCA observer status, and in April 2011, in Singapore, this application was unanimously endorsed by the ICCA Steering Committee. Cal Dooley, president and CEO of the ACC and president of the ICCA Steering Committee, wrote to Al- Sadoun, extending warm praise for the lead taken by the GPCA in implementing Responsible Care in the Arabian Gulf region:

> The GPCA's comprehensive approach to developing and implementing a Responsible Care program serves as a model for associations that want to join ICCA. I am pleased that the ACC has been able to play a small role in the GPCA's development of such a world-class program.

In 2012, ICCA ranked the GPCA at the top among fifty-five global associations with regard to Responsible Care. Noting the tremendous strides the GPCA had made in implementing the Responsible Care initiative in the Arabian Gulf region, on 5 June 2012, the ICCA Board approved the GPCA's application for "full membership," and on 27 September 2012 in London, this decision was unanimously confirmed by the ICCA General Assembly. This made the GPCA the youngest organization ever to achieve such a status within a period of two years, and it was a testimony to the GPCA's enormous progress in getting member companies to implement Responsible Care. The ICCA Board agreed to designate a seat on its Board of Directors, effective January 2013, for a CEO representing the GPCA. This position was taken by GPCA's then chairman, Mohamed Al-Mady.

Human Resource Development

The GPCA's Human Resources Committee had been created at the very outset and was to be précised on 1 March 2007. Chaired by Yusuf Ebrahim Fakhroo of the GPIC, it was formed in response to concerns that the pool of talent available to the Arabian Gulf petrochemical industry was inadequate despite the industry's best efforts. This made expansion difficult.

The human resource challenge was a topic of discussion at the GPCA's first Annual Forum in December 2006. "There is a diminishing pool of skilled labor, and experts are predicting a crunch in 2008–2009. A forum like GPCA is imperative in tackling these concerns in a collective and consensual manner," predicted Paul Eccleston, CEO of the Contax Group, UAE.

Meeting manpower needs by training local people to operate and run petrochemical facilities had been an essential part of joint-venture agreements with Western partners in the Gulf for several decades, but such training was never enough.

To address these issues, the Human Resources Committee organized a range of activities. In 2008, it ran a talent management workshop, which focused on how the success of a company is dependent on having the right talent at the right place at the right time and in the right quantity to execute its strategies; it commissioned an EQUATE-led survey on remuneration and benefits packages for executive and nonexecutive staff; it organized a breakout session on human resources issues during the Annual Forum; it participated in an event to strengthen ties between academic institutions and the corporate world; and it compiled a list of offsite meetings for member companies to aid transparency and share best practices.

In 2009, the committee's theme was leadership. It held a workshop in Kuwait ("Leading in Hard Times"); it started to develop a "competency catalogue" dictionary to be accessible through the GPCA website; and it invited Vijay Govindarajan of the Tuck School of Business at Dartmouth College to speak on leadership at the breakout session during the fourth Annual GPCA Forum, as well as to take part in a panel discussion. It explored the idea of an employee exchange program to allow members to provide support services to each other, and promoted sharing and exchange of resources and knowledge. In June 2009, the GPCA board appointed board member Maha Mulla Hussain as the committee chair, with Abeer Al-Omar of EQUATE retained as the committee's vice chair.

Adding "retention of talent" to its theme of leadership, in 2010, the committee organized two main workshops and asked consultants to facilitate a session on organizational effectiveness. On 9–11 October 2011, it launched its first GPCA Talent Convention in Dubai, which gave local and regional industry executives a platform to present their knowledge in the fields of strategic organizational capabilities, talent development, and management. A second convention took place on 16–18 October the next year.

Plastics

Early on, the GPCA's board saw the need to have an Industrial Committee. When the time came, two committees were created, one dealing with plastics and the other with logistics. Both became operational by mid-2008.

EQUATE's Adel Al-Munifi first chaired the Plastics Committee (July 2008–January 2009), which worked to counter a growing effort in the Arabian Gulf region to "condemn plastics as a public health hazard and a major cause of environmental pollution." It was feared that this effort would lead states in the region to ban plastic carrier bags. In 2010, Al-Sadoun observed that the public image of plastics had been under pressure in recent years, and the GPCA was responding by bringing to public attention the many benefits and advantages of plastics.

The Plastics Committee, now under the chairmanship of Muayad Al Faresi, communicated to the public the "significant contributions of plastics in our day-to-day life." Using "comprehensive, science-based policies," it sought to "redefine the image of plastics, promote plastics as a responsible material choice, and highlight the positive role of the plastics industry and plastics materials in the community."

The committee engaged a global consulting firm, Ri*Questa GmbH, to conduct a regional "plastic image survey" to discover public perceptions and acceptance of plastics in the six GCC states. This survey was the first implementation of an approach that the GPCA has subsequently used extensively, which is gathering and using data to tackle key issues. The survey found that Gulf citizens and residents generally had a "strongly favorable attitude" to the plastics industry and plastics products. Anti-plastics sentiment related mainly to litter and waste management.

In 2009, the committee began to promote the "four Rs": responsible use, reuse, recycle, and recover. It promoted enforcement of littering laws and campaigned for opportunities and facilities to recycle plastics and to recover the energy embedded in plastic products. It also evolved a multifaceted program to address public concerns about plastics and to raise awareness about the benefits they brought to communities. The GPCA appointed "plastics ambassadors" who promoted the "virtues and value" of plastics, emphasizing the positive role of plastics in reducing pollution and the expenditure of resources.

Realizing the importance of working with decision makers, the committee began to liaise with retail chains in the UAE, Qatar, and Saudi Arabia on issues such as waste management and the use of plastic bags. As time went on, the committee—representing the voice of industry—began to engage governmental and regional agencies to press for the adoption and implementation of appropriate regulations and standards related to plastics.

Following an initial workshop, in 2009, the Plastics Committee also organized three subsequent workshops on waste management, with support from Plastics

Abdulaziz Alhajri, chairman of the Plastics Committee from 2012 to 2015.

Europe. It presented a paper at the GPCA's Annual Forum and sent a representative to the Global Plastics Meeting, in Arlington, Virginia, as part of a process of wider participation.

In alignment with a board resolution that required all committees to be chaired by a board member, Al-Qurtas became in 2010 the chairman of the Plastics Committee, with Al Faresi retained as the committee vice chairman. In June 2010, the committee stepped up its work by holding the GPCA's First Plastics Summit in Dubai. The event focused on sustainability across the value chain and argued that plastics are critical to modern life. Through its efforts, the Plastics Committee had been actively advocating that "plastics needn't be seen as the enemy. Rather, it is people's attitude toward plastics that poses the danger."

This is aligned with the second area of focus for the committee: to assist in developing a globally competitive plastic conversion industry in the GCC region. To that end, in 2011, the committee introduced the GPCA Plastic Innovation Awards, which recognized the regional plastic converters who made important innovations. The awards were presented in a special ceremony addressed by the GPCA chairman, Mohamed Al-Mady.

In 2012, Al-Qurtas stepped down from the chairmanship of the committee to lead the Research and Innovation area. He was replaced by Abdulaziz Alhajri, CEO of Borouge, with Rashid Al Ghurair, CEO of Taghleef, taking the role of the committee's vice chairman. This step reflected the GPCA's increasing effort to engage the leaders of the Plastic Conversion industry in shaping the direction of the Plastics Committee. Parallel to that, the GPCA secretariat redrafted the committee charter in 2010 to allocate one-third of its membership to plastics convertors and resins additives producers.

On 27 February 2013, the GPCA launched its first annual community awareness campaign to highlight issues associated with "plastic waste management" and "littering" and the need for the community to unite and respond to this problem.

Conducted in all the GCC cities, the first campaign was called "Clean Up the Gulf." In 2014, the Plastics Committee renamed it "Waste Free Environment." The campaign has overall been a grand success, as demonstrated by the participation of 18,909 volunteers, over 190 schools, and 405 divers, who collected solid waste from the water. In its first three years, the campaign collected 73.7 tons of waste, leading to the recycling of 35 percent of the plastics gathered. In 2015, the campaign expanded its geographical coverage beyond the GCC region to cover sites in which GPCA members operate, including Mumbai in India and Sittard-Geleen in the Netherlands.

The Plastics Committee also collaborated with consulting firms to develop cobranded reports with Nexant that focused on key issues for petrochemical producers and plastics converters. These reports included *GCC Plastics Processing Industry* (2013) and *A New Horizon for the GCC Plastics Processing Industry* (2015).

Volunteers gather for the GPCA's Clean Up the Gulf Initiative.

Logistics and Supply-Chain Management

Being predominantly export oriented, logistics had long been recognized as a critical issue for the petrochemical industry in the Arabian Gulf. Hence, it is not surprising that the Logistics Committee was among the first that the GPCA created. In July 2009, the name was changed to Supply Chain Committee, and Walid Al-Hammad of Tasnee was named its chairman.

Through the committee, the association hoped to get member companies involved in improving the regional supply chain. One of the committee's initial achievements was to map out a three-year strategy, including plans to organize a regular supply-chain forum that would bring together petrochemical and chemical companies, supply-chain service providers, storage and packaging companies, and government authorities—such as ministries, ports, free zones, and terminal operators.

The committee's first event was a breakout session in December 2008 at the GPCA's third Annual Forum. The first GPCA Supply Chain Conference followed in October 2009 in Bahrain and attracted a number of prestigious speakers, leading the committee to pledge to make the conference an annual event. The committee also set up dedicated workshops to emphasize the need to adopt global supply-chain management standards in the Gulf.

In addition, the committee worked to identify important areas for improvement, while also promoting relevant research, benchmarking studies, information sharing, and the standardization of safety regulations for handling and transporting products. In light of the key role played by the service providers in this industry's functional area, the GPCA secretariat redrafted the committee charter in 2010 to allocate one-third of its membership to logistics and supply-chain companies.

In 2010, as well as organizing a second Supply Chain Conference, the committee published a comprehensive study focusing on the GCC and Iran titled "The Gulf Supply Chain Landscape, 2005–2015" and established a task force, with help from a consultant, to consolidate supply-chain management information for GPCA members.

In June 2009, the GPCA board had appointed its vice chairman, Hamad Al-Terkait, to chair the Supply Chain Committee, with Abdulaziz Al-Bati of Tasnee retained as the committee's vice chair. In 2012, the committee's management was changed with Mohammad Husain, the incoming CEO of EQUATE, becoming chairman and Saleh Al-Shabnan, vice president at SABIC, becoming vice chairman.

In 2013, in order to provide a rich program for the GPCA Supply Chain Conferences, the committee opted to engage A. T. Kearney as a "content partner."

The Supply Chain Committee also partnered with leading consultancy firms to produce the following industry relevant cobranded reports:

- *Horn of Africa Piracy and the Gulf Petrochemical Industry* (cobranded report with A. T. Kearney, 2011);

- *Managing Supply Chain Risk: Understanding Piracy Threat* (cobranded study with A. T. Kearney, 2012);

- *Supply Chain Talent Management in the Arabian Gulf* (cobranded report with Accenture, 2013; in Arabic and English);

- *Gulf Rail Connection—Realizing the GCC Economic Unity* (cobranded report with A. T. Kearney, 2013; in Arabic and English); and

- *GCC Women in Supply Chain (cobranded report with Accenture, 2015; in Arabic and English).*

Increasing Scope

In 2009, the board debated and endorsed the proposal of the secretary general to create two more committees: a Fertilizer Committee and an Advocacy Committee. The latter was set up in August 2009 to represent the regional industry on trade and public policy issues. Board member Ahmad Al-Ohali, CEO of Sipchem, was its chairman, with Abdullah Al-Sadhan, general manager at SABIC, as vice chairman. The committee sought to address international trade matters, ensure fair competition, support the GPCA's goals and objectives in protecting the industry's lawful interests, and provide guidance to its members on trade issues and other business challenges. It held several capacity-building workshops to educate GPCA members about antidumping practices, international trade policy, and the regulations of the World Trade Organization. It also engaged with the consulting firm Nexant to develop two cobranded reports: *The Role of GCC Fertilizers in Addressing Food Security* (2014) and *Global Fertilizer Trends, Opportunities, and Challenges* (2013).

The Advocacy Committee came into being as India—and later China and the European Union—began to impose antidumping duties primarily directed at Saudi Arabia and Oman, both producers of polypropylene. The GPCA was at the forefront of addressing this clear threat to the Arabian Gulf industry. It retained a team of international legal consultants to give advice on the matter and develop criteria for tariff exemptions. Having taken "a strong stand" on antidumping, the GPCA vowed to work with GCC governments to ensure "that exports of petrochemicals and chemicals from the Arabian Gulf region are not restricted by antidumping or other trade restrictions." It described the actions of India and China to penalize GGC producers as "protectionist measures in the garb of antidumping procedures."

In December 2009, following a GPCA seminar on fertilizers, the Fertilizers Committee was formed. As was the case with other committees, it soon had plans to develop its own conference, database, and capacity workshops. The first event was a technical workshop covering topics relating to fertilizer production, which took place in May 2010 in Bahrain. The GPCA Board of Directors quickly approved plans for an annual fertilizer conference, which would allow producers to continue to exchange ideas, discuss challenges, and benefit from shared knowledge. The committee also developed a support network for the benefit of the GPCA's member companies.

Routinizing Success

The year 2009 had proved to be one of extensive GPCA activities. In addition to its Annual Forum and the work of its committees, the association held its first Supply Chain Conference in October 2009 and also carried out a range of workshops. "The GPCA is advancing toward its ambitious goals," reported *Chemical Week*. One small but key decision of the board in 2009 had been to require that each committee be chaired by a board member. This change aimed to facilitate fast-track decisions and "help ensure high-level involvement and direction." This action was coupled with structural changes that the GPCA's new secretary general, Abdulwahab Al-Sadoun, had proposed with regard to the committees.

In 2010, the pace quickened as the GPCA worked intensively on sharing information, introducing best practices, and encouraging transparency. GPCA member companies were becoming ever more deeply involved in committee activities by providing experts to speak at workshops and by sending representatives

Fertilizer Conference.

REACH workshop.

to sit on the actual committees. "Our committees will continue to address important issues facing our industry through dialogue and workshops," Al-Mady told an interviewer. Committees were plainly yielding increasing benefits for members.

One need was expeditious implementation of the Responsible Care initiative. In 2011, the Responsible Care Committee created seven task forces entrusted with the job of developing codes. The first three codes developed related to distribution, chemical awareness and emergency response (CAER), and product stewardship. Management practices vis-à-vis these three codes then became the focus of a two-day workshop, which was facilitated by representatives of the ACC.

The new Research and Innovation Committee, formed in 2012, was dedicated to heightening awareness of the value of research and innovation in developing a sustainable future for the industry in the region. Chaired by Moayyed Al-Qurtas of Tasnee, the committee briskly gathered R&D data for each GCC country, organized workshops on intellectual property management, and prepared for the GPCA's First Research and Innovation Summit, which took place on 12–13 March 2014. It sought to encourage a research and innovation culture and the adoption of best practices in innovation management.

With formulation of the new strategy for the association in 2012, among other changes, the task of advocating was assigned to each committee. As a result, the Advocacy Committee became the International Trade Committee, chaired by Ahmad Al-Ohali of Sipchem and charged with addressing a growing number of antidumping and antisubsidy cases that targeted the industry in the Gulf. The committee adopted four objectives: 1) to build awareness of antidumping measures and antitrust laws; 2) to monitor international trade practices and trade

The formation of the GPCA was the dream of founders of the petrochemical industry in the Arabian Gulf countries. We wanted a platform to discuss issues of mutual interest and to exchange knowledge. In ten years, the founders and members of the GPCA were not only able to realize their dream but to exceed it by forming one of the world's most respected chemical organizations. It can now attract over 2,200 professionals and decision makers to its Annual Forum. Advocacy, Responsible Care, supply chain, and sustainability are at the forefront of GPCA's business activities.

—*Abdulrahman Jawahery, founding board member of GPCA and CEO of Gulf Petrochemical Industry Company*

policy, focusing on regulatory measures that might affect the access of GCC producers to markets; 3) to promote the GPCA's positions through publications; and 4) to serve as the voice for GPCA members and represent their interests vis-à-vis regional and international trade bodies, intergovernmental organizations, and such trade associations as ACC, ICCA, CEFIC, and the International Fertilizer Industry Association.

By now it was clear to everyone, whether GPCA member or outside observer, that the association was a powerful, credible, and successful force. And its committees were a key part of its due diligence, knowledge, and influence.

5 The Annual Forum and Other Major Events

Humble Beginnings

When chairman Mohamed Al-Mady announced to the world the formation of the GPCA, its founders had already decided that conferences would be central to its raison d'être. Moreover, they determined that such events would address global industry issues and gather speakers and delegates from outside the region as well as from the GCC. Despite its having a staff of just three people, the association made fast work of planning its GPCA Annual Forum: the first event the GPCA had ever planned! Few then would have imagined that in fewer than ten years, the GPCA Annual Forum would become the premier networking hub for the global petrochemical industry.

As Al-Mady reflects,

> We dared to hold our first Annual Forum in less than nine months, in December 2006. That's the way it has always been at GPCA. We set ambitious objectives and then set about organizing the infrastructure to achieve them.

The first Annual Forum was a great success by any standard. Over four hundred industry professionals from around the world gathered in Dubai to attend the two-day forum, where they discussed industry issues and pursued commercial opportunities. True to GPCA's intent to focus the Annual Forum on global issues, forum organizers recruited a strong lineup of speakers that included leading executives from ExxonMobil Chemicals, Shell Chemicals, and Borealis, who presented their views on such issues as feedstocks, the rapid increase in investment in the region, the need to enhance logistics and infrastructure to cope with burgeoning export volumes, and the development of downstream user industries in Middle Eastern countries.

The first forum, the region's largest gathering ever of its kind, set a template for years to come. The GPCA's first secretary general, Abdullah Al-Hagbani, heralded the inaugural forum as "our organization's flagship event, and the first of many gatherings to provide insight into key issues impacting our dynamic and fast-growing industry." In the next years, the Annual Forum would attract ever more impressive rosters of speakers—CEOs of leading companies in Europe,

Ribbon cutting at the GPCA's first Annual Forum. *From left to right, front row*: Moayyed Al-Qurtas, Abdullah Al-Hagbani, Mohamed Al-Mady, Hamad Al-Terkait, and Abdulrahman Jawahery.

Asia, the United States, and the Arabian Gulf region. No other event in the world would secure so many CEOs of major companies as speakers. When the GPCA first conceived the Annual Forum, its hope was that the event would attract more than a thousand delegates by 2010—a goal it easily surpassed.

The GPCA's first Annual Forum was held at the Habtoor Grand Hotel, Dubai, and opened on 16 December 2006 under the title "Developments and Opportunities in the GCC's Petrochemical and Chemical Sectors." The speakers included the GPCA's own Mohamed Al-Mady (SABIC), Hamad Al-Terkait (EQUATE), Hubert Puchner (Borouge), Abdulrahman Jawahery (GPIC), and Hamad Al-Mohannadi (QAPCO). Among speakers from companies outside the Arabian Gulf region were Michael J. Dolan (ExxonMobil), Frances Keeth (Shell), Khalid Al-Falih (Saudi Aramco), and Otto Fritzer (Stolt-Neilsen).

Building the Reality

In succeeding years, the Annual Forum has gone from strength to strength. In March 2007, GPCA directors selected *Chemical Week* as the forum's main co-organizer. The theme of the second Annual Forum, held at the Grand Hyatt Dubai Hotel, was "Fulfilling Global Aspirations as a Strategic Partner." Forum

Chairman and vice chairman of the GPCA, Mohamed Al-Mady and Hamad Al-Terkait, sit side by side at the GPCA's inaugural meeting in 2006.

organizers had aimed at attracting 750 participants. Instead, they drew 838, nearly double the number of participants from the year before.

Al-Terkait was able to emphasize the "huge networking opportunity" the forum provided and the opportunity it offered to keep abreast of developments. Al-Mady described the forum as one of the pivotal events in the global petrochemicals calendar and the most important activity for the GPCA. In his opening address, he spoke of rising project construction costs in the Middle East and overbuilding accompanied by weaker markets. He was positive about the industry's inherent strengths, as it works through periods of overcapacity and slow growth and emerges stronger.

The forum's panel of speakers resembled a Who's Who of the global petrochemical industry and included a stellar retinue of leaders from outside of the Gulf: Mukesh Ambani of Reliance, Raymond Wilcox of Chevron Phillips Chemical Company, Peter Huntsman of Huntsman Corporation, Stephanie Burns of Dow Corning, Andrew Liveris of Dow Chemical, and Volker Trautz of Basell, to name a few. The Annual Forum emerged in 2007 as one of the most sought-after events of the petrochemical industry and a major networking opportunity, even as storm clouds gathered ominously, foreshadowing the Great Recession.

In 2008, the association expanded its networking opportunities. Prompted by the activities of its committees, which were busy identifying and raising issues of common concern, the GPCA ran several workshops. The association's "constant endeavor" was to create "more and more opportunities for interaction among the member companies." That year also saw the planning of many smaller annual get-togethers to focus on specific issues and industry sectors.

However, by now the world was going through an economic crisis. The Gulf was not unscathed. At the November 2008 Annual Forum, petrochemical industry watchers were speaking of tough challenges ahead, but the GPCA itself ended the year on a high note as leaders and managers from around the globe gathered again in Dubai. Given the GPCA's growing stature and the success of the Annual Forum the previous year, it is not surprising that the Annual Forum in 2008 attracted more participants than in 2007. Dubai and the GPCA were accessible, organized, and attractive.

Ray Wilcox, CEO of Chevron Phillips Chemical Company, addresses the second GPCA Forum.

At the fourth Annual GPCA Forum, Mohamed Al-Mady was joined by the GPCA's new secretary general, Abdulwahab Al-Sadoun.

With the theme "Managing Growth and Competitiveness in a Cyclical Industry," 950 participants heard from Abdullah Bin Hamad Al-Attiyah, the deputy prime minister of Qatar and chairman of Qatar Petroleum, Abdulrahman Jawahery of GPIC, Jeffrey Lipton of Nova Chemical, Ben van Beurden of Shell Chemicals, Li Xihong of Sinopec, Jose Carlos Grubisich of Bioenergia, and Florian Budde of McKinsey. Hassan Ahmed of HSBC Securities gave a talk entitled "The Financial Crisis: Where Does the Global Chemical Sector Go from Here?"

The year 2009 was capped by the fourth Annual GPCA Forum that despite the ongoing recession attracted over a thousand participants. The theme was "Breaking through the Crisis to Pursue Sustainable Growth." Speakers from outside of the Arabian Gulf region included Stephen Pryor of ExxonMobil Chemical, Klaus Engel of Evonik, Greg Garland of Chevron Phillips Chemical, Mark Garrett of Borealis, and Brad Bourland of Jadwa Investments.

The highlight of the fourth Annual Forum was a keynote speech from the Saudi oil minister, Ali Al-Naimi, who spoke of the Gulf's continuing dominance and emphasized that despite global financial strains, the overall economy of the Gulf region remained strong. He noted that many challenges remained in the areas of manpower and innovation, but urged companies to continue to provide training to further upgrade and burnish the skills of their workforce. He also called on companies in the Gulf to look for ways to separate themselves from competitors through innovation and development of proprietary technology and markets. The Gulf's chemicals industry, Al-Naimi contended, needed to redouble its efforts in environmental stewardship, corporate social responsibility, training and employment of nationals, promotion of R&D to support new technologies and small businesses, and best practices and corporate governance.

The GPCA's fifth Annual Forum took place from 7 to 9 December 2010 at the Intercontinental Festival City in Dubai. The steady increase in the number of participants continued, with 1,350 delegates from around the world participating. The theme of 2010 was "Driving Value and Growth through Innovation." Sheikha Lubna Al Qasimi, minister of foreign trade for the UAE, opened the

The Gala Dinner at the fifth Annual Forum provided a wonderful opportunity for networking. *Right:* Khalid Al-Falih has been a frequent speaker at the GPCA Annual Forum; here he addresses delegates at the fifth Annual Forum and foresees a fivefold increase in petrochemical revenues in the GCC by 2020.

event, and Abdulwahab Al-Sadoun presented the results of the GPCA's innovation survey. Khalid Al-Falih of Saudi Aramco called for a decade of transition to achieve dramatic growth and diversification, and identified three enablers: R&D, human resource development, and the cultivation of a dynamic environment for commercial success. Other leading speakers at the forum included Victor Chu of Far Eastern Investment Group, David Weidman of Celanese, Ki-Joon Hong of Hanwha Chemical Corporation, Dmitry Konov of Sibur, Rainer Diercks of BASF SE, Christian Jourquin of Solvay, Axel Heitmann of Lanxess, François Cornélis of Total, and the GPCA's own Mohamed Al-Mady.

For the first time, the association organized a seminar on the sidelines of its main forum, entitled "Chemical Market Outlook," to encourage interactivity. More than four hundred attended this event, designed to harness the expertise, analytics, and knowledge available and share it with delegates in a program focused on educating professionals in trends and core concepts. Overall, the forum carried two clear messages: that the Arabian Gulf would consolidate its strategic position in the global industry through further growth, and that the region was serious about building a solid structural framework to nurture a culture of innovation.

The sixth Annual Forum was held from 13 to 15 December 2011 at Dubai's Atlantis Hotel. Themed "Moving Downstream: Creating Added Value and Sustainable Growth," the forum gave industry leaders a platform to showcase opportunities to capture the added value currently being exported by building major downstream industries. The keynote speaker was Prince Faisal bin Turki Al-Saud, adviser at Saudi Arabia's Ministry of Petroleum and Mineral Resources who urged the region's players to focus on adopting innovative approaches, support

Abdulaziz Al-Zamil and other delegates pass through an archway
flanked by dancers at the banquet for the sixth Annual GPCA
Forum.

development of globally competitive downstream industries, and encourage the
development of local talent.

Among the other speakers were Hamad Al-Mohannadi of Qatar Petroleum,
Stephen Pryor of ExxonMobil, James Gallogly of LyondellBasell, and Peter L.
Cella of Chevron Phillips. On the sidelines, two seminars dealt with markets and
feedstocks." The forum's "profile, content, and outcome" were strengthening
steadily.

The seventh Annual Forum was held at the Jumeirah Mandinat in Dubai
and focused on the theme "Sustaining Competitiveness in a Rapidly Changing
World." The opening address was provided by the UAE minister of environment
and water, Rashid Bin Fahad, and the keynote speaker was Choon Fong Shih,
then president of King Abdullah University of Science and Technology.

Two topics dominated the conference: innovation and shale gas. In his
address to the forum, Mohamed Al-Mady, then chairman of GPCA, stressed the
need to improve innovation activities. CEOs from U.S., European, Asian, and
South American companies echoed this perspective. With regard to the development of shale gas reserves in the United States, the consensus of presenters was
that this was a significant "game changer" and required analysis to determine its
impact on the industry in various parts of the world.

The eighth Annual Forum was held from 19 to 21 November 2013 at Ma-
dinat Jumeirah with the theme "Innovation: The Foundation of Chemical Value
Chain Leadership." The inaugural address was made by Prince Abdulaziz bin Salman Al-Saud, the undersecretary at the Saudi Ministry of Petroleum and Minerals.
The forum featured such industry leaders as SABIC's Mohamed Al-Mady,

ExxonMobil's Stephen Pryor, LyondellBasell's James Gallogly, Indorama's Aloke Lohia, and Teijin's Shigeo Ohyagi. The forum attracted nearly two thousand participants, continuing the steady growth in the scope and popularity of the Annual Forum.

The ninth Annual Forum, held 23 to 25 November 2014, met with even more success. With the theme "The Strategic Direction of the Chemical Industry," it attracted over 2,100 delegates from forty countries, who listened to the leaders of major global chemical companies speak to such topics as facing challenges through innovation (Patrick Thomas, CEO of Bayer Material Science); leading with innovation (Thomas Connelly Jr., executive vice president of DuPont); and sustainable growth (Peter Cella, CEO of Chevron Phillips Chemical). After a plenary address by Mohammed bin Saleh al Sada, minister of energy and industry in Qatar, two keynote speakers, Khalid Al-Falih, CEO of Aramco, and Andrew Liveris, CEO of Dow Chemical, spoke about the Dow-Aramco joint venture, Sadara, and how it is ambitiously integrating the entire value chain. Liveris

The rapid development of the GPCA has been driven by the strong engagement of the founding members, by the leadership of local member companies, and by the excellent staff and leadership at the GPCA. The GPCA has demonstrated thought leadership, as seen through the ever-growing and improving quality of reports and availability of industry data. It has also demonstrated an ability to deliver initiatives, such as the rapid implementation of Responsible Care, and it has partnered effectively with others, be it with the news media, consulting companies, the Society of Plastic Engineers, and other associations around the world to rapidly learn, adopt, and share best practices. This has led to the GPCA's rapid admission to the International Council of Chemical Associations. The GPCA is also an important organization supporting the image and reputation of our industry. Its Waste Free Environment day is a good example of this reputation building, an event that LyondellBasell has been proud to play a lead role in establishing and sponsoring.

—*Bhavesh Patel, CEO of LyondellBasell*

Abdullah Bin Hamad Al Attiyah, deputy prime minister and minister of energy of Qatar, and the keynote speaker at the third Annual Forum.

Ali bin Ibrahim Al-Naimi, minister of petroleum and mineral resources of Saudi Arabia and the keynote speaker at the fourth Annual Forum.

Sheikha Lubna Al Qasimi, minister of international cooperation and development of the UAE, and keynote speaker at the fifth Annual Forum.

Prince Faisal bin Turki Al-Saud, advisor, Ministry of Petroleum and Minerals of Saudi Arabia, and the keynote speaker at the sixth Annual Forum.

Rashid Bin Fahad, minister of environment and water of the UAE, and the keynote speaker at the seventh Annual Forum.

Prince Abdulaziz bin Salman Al-Saud, deputy minister for petroleum of Saudi Arabia, and the keynote speaker at the eighth Annual Forum.

Mohammed bin Saleh al Sada, minister of energy and industry of Qatar, and the keynote speaker at the ninth Annual Forum.

Panel discussion at the First Annual Forum. *From left to right:* Khalid Al-Falih of Aramco, Hamad Al-Terkait of EQUATE, Philip Leighton of Jacobs Consultancy, Muttaq Al-Morished of SABIC, and Paul Eccleston of the Contax Group.

FIGURE 2. GPCA Annual Forum Attendance, 2006–2014

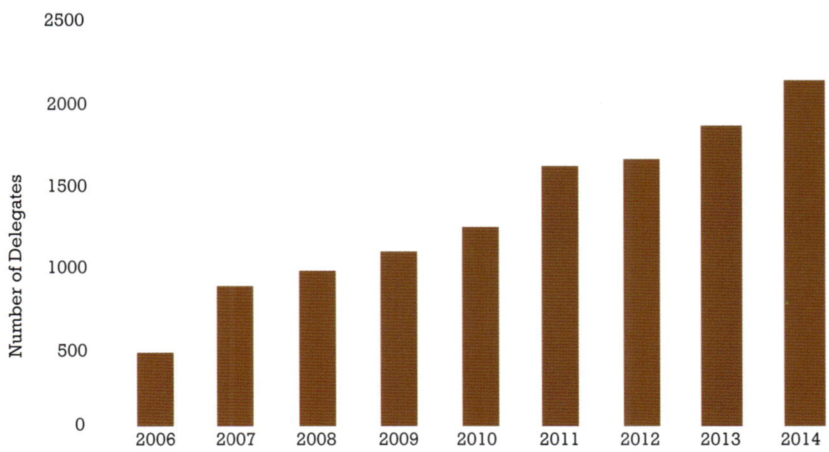

noted that although shale gas from the United States is reshaping the competitive landscape around the world, "the fact that Dow is also a major investor in Saudi Arabia proves that today's world is too big to rely on any one region for its growing feedstock needs" (Figure 2).

Committee-Related Networking and Educational Events

As the Annual Forum evolved, the committees of the GPCA also began to organize conferences, summits, and other "signature events" focused on issues of significance to the regional petrochemical community. They were as follows:

- Supply Chain Conference

- Plastic Summit (renamed PlastiCon in 2012)

- Fertilizer Convention

- Sustainability Conference

- Research and Innovation Summit

- Responsible Care Conference

A Plethora of Platforms

As the GPCA continued to expand its portfolio of events, many of its smaller conferences became highly successful in their own right, attracting speakers and delegates from around the world. The calendar became steadily busier from the start of 2010 as the global economy began to recover. That June, the GPCA's Plastics Committee held the association's first Plastics Summit, in Dubai. Conferees discussed the image of plastics and prospects for downstream Arabian Gulf

Moayyed Al-Qurtas, CEO of Tasnee, addresses delegates at the first Conference on Plastic Conversion in 2010.

investment. Recycling was an issue of concern, and speakers called for more initiatives in the GCC countries.

Two events quickly followed. The first was the GPCA's initial Fertilizer Convention, held in September at the InterContinental Festival City in Dubai. Its theme was "Working toward Food Security: Forecasting Fertilizers Demand—Strategies for Supply." Satish Chander (Fertilizer Association of India) spoke on the long-term fertilizer needs of India, by far the largest market for GCC fertilizer producers. More than two hundred delegates attended from over thirty countries. The event enabled participants to assess market conditions and capacity planning and to discuss ways to enhance food security. There were "passionate calls" to invest in a next generation of fertilizers to help the world reduce the use of land and water resources, while boosting output and lessening environmental impact.

The second event, co-organized by *Chemical Week*, was the GPCA's second Supply Chain Conference. Held in Bahrain, it was preceded by a one-day workshop on regional standards, facilitated by the Chemical Distribution Institute. The conference itself attracted over two hundred industry leaders and experts who heard from twelve speakers. The insights generated would help foster the adoption of uniform supply-chain standards and practices.

It was not just the GPCA calendar that was busy: all three subsidiary forums—supply-chain management, plastics, and fertilizers—were by now "firm fixtures on the calendars of industry executives in the Gulf and worldwide." They had become "vibrant platforms for exchanging ideas, information, and knowledge as well as for business networking, all at the senior level. "We strive to create the right platform," said Al-Sadoun, "where issues relevant to strategic industry can be discussed and debated.

GPCA Awards

In 2011, the GPCA launched its awards program. Believing healthy competition could foster good practices and raise standards in the industry, the association envisaged a series of awards to encourage excellence and recognize industry

Ziad Al-Labban addresses the second Plastics Summit as the keynote speaker.

success stories. The first awards were for plastics innovation and were coupled with the second Plastics Summit, held in April 2011 in Dubai. These Plastics Innovation Awards had four categories (products, conversion processing, environment, and talents) and were designed to underline "the commitment of GPCA member companies to develop and support regional downstream industries" and recognize advancements that generated a positive impact on society. The award recipients were Green Vision from Saudi Arabia, for its innovative and ecofriendly turf system; Zamil Plastics from Saudi Arabia, for developing a holistic system to convert non-plastic parts to plastic parts; Taghleef Industries of Dubai, for its BoPLA (biodegradable biaxially oriented polylacetic acid) sustainable packaging film; and Mohammed Al-Ghamdi and Krishna Prasad Rajan of Yanbu Industrial College in Saudi Arabia, for their development of environmentally friendly, completely biodegradable biocomposites materials.

Plastics Excellence Awards recipients at the fourth Conference on Plastic Conversion in 2013.

The colorful Plastics Award is an important GPCA recognition of excellence.

Another important event of the year was the second Fertilizer Convention, held in September in Doha on the theme "Growth in Volatile Markets." Some 260 people attended from 36 countries. Mohammed bin Saleh al Sada, minister of energy and industry of Qatar, gave the opening address; and U. S. Awasthi of the India Farmers Fertilizer Cooperative gave a keynote speech. Nexant's Andrew Prince closed the conference by offering insights into factors that would contribute to volatility in urea markets around the world.

The year 2011 also saw the GPCA's first Talent Convention, held in Dubai in October: a two-day program for human resource professionals, it attracted 150 delegates. Maha Mulla Hussain, chair of the GPCA's Human Resources Committee, gave a welcome address, and among the speakers was Donald Sull of the London Business School. The focus of the event was women in leadership roles. Through such events and conventions, the GPCA was fulfilling its objective for knowledge sharing among members, organizing "multiple learning platforms." Through its committees, it also ran dedicated workshops—including two each on fertilizers, advocacy, and industry leadership—that enabled its members to discuss opportunities for growth, development, and prosperity.

Maha Mulla Hussain, former managing director and chair of the Petrochemical Industry Company of Kuwait, and former member of the GPCA board.

In 2012, the GPCA continued both to evolve and to grow. April saw the opening of the third Plastics Summit on the theme "Plastics Conversion: Growth Opportunities in Challenging Markets." The summit attracted 350 delegates and included the second Plastics Innovation Awards. The fourth Supply Chain Conference took place in May in Dubai. Its theme was "Optimization through Collaboration," and it attracted more than 275 senior industry representatives from 95 companies. Mohammed Al Muallem of DP World was the keynote speaker, and Mohammad Husain, CEO of EQUATE and the new chair of the GPCA's Supply Chain Committee, spoke of challenges, including port congestion, inadequate infrastructure, and instability of market conditions.

In September 2012, the GPCA's third Fertilizer Convention welcomed Rashid Bin Fahad, the UAE minister of environment and water, as guest of honor. The Talent Convention, rebranded the second Human Capital Convention, took place the following month.

The rapid growth of the GPCA can be attributed to its visionary leadership. The eight founding members of the GPCA, EQUATE being one of them, envisioned that the GPCA could play a role as a regional platform for sharing knowledge and exchange of best practices among its members and other stakeholders. The sustained growth of the GPCA is a reflection of the members commitment toward "Sustained Cooperation" between themselves and their global peers. The common interest and shared values and vision of the regional industry's leadership has laid the foundation for the rapid and sustainable development of the GPCA.

—*Mohammad Husain, CEO of EQUATE and current member of GPCA's board*

6 The GPCA Today

A New Strategy

In 2010, the GPCA began to grapple seriously with the strategies needed to build on its remarkable success, as the faltering global economy finally showed hints of renewed growth. The association had already far exceeded its initial modest goals. Now it wanted to capitalize on its strengths as it looked to the future.

In October, the GPCA Board of Directors met with consultants from McKinsey and Company. In a workshop setting, they discussed strategic topics, with an emphasis on the importance of leadership development (both individually and by company cooperation) in an increasingly competitive landscape. In October 2011, the board considered formal proposals that had been submitted by A. T. Kearney, Stratley, and Booz and Company—to develop an overall strategy for the GPCA.

A.T. Kearney's strategic vision in many ways echoed the one that Al-Sadoun had presented in 2009. It noted that the GPCA's global reputation was built on its networking events, headed by the Annual Forum and augmented by the success of GPCA summits, conferences, and workshops. Kearney suggested that the association leverage its networking position to develop its advocacy role. In this way, the GPCA would position itself as a network-advocate association, similar to the ACC and CEFIC. The consultants also suggested that the GPCA serve more as a source of valuable information to the industry—in other words, take on the role of a think tank. To follow this path, the GPCA would need to increase its staff and expand the level of staff expertise, for example, securing staff with legal expertise (Figure 3). A. T. Kearney also recommended adding an Innovation Committee to the GPCA's roster of working committees. The GPCA board endorsed engaging A. T. Kearney to assist with the association's strategic planning. It also acted on some of the firm's initial suggestions, for example, creating an Innovation and Research Committee to supplant the Human Resources Committee.

A. T. Kearney's first steps in the strategic project were to interview stakeholders and to benchmark the association against its international peers. In June 2012, A. T. Kearney came back to the directors with three scenarios for the GPCA's future role, entailing its evolution either as a "global networker," "GCC

FIGURE 3. Growth of GPCA Staff, 2006–2015

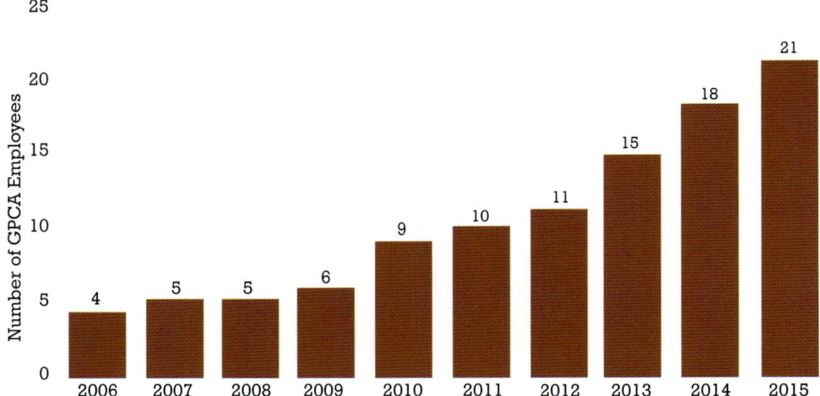

shaper," or "GCC driver." The board chose the third option, which would entail a broader geographical focus with increased efforts in networking, advocacy, and think-tank activities. The annual report for 2012 affirmed the GPCA's chosen strategic direction:

> The GPCA continues to provide excellent networking opportunities, such as the Annual Forum, for its member companies. Through ensuring that key themes and priorities are embedded in these events, synergies between the three pillars can be realized. GPCA's strong networking position can be leveraged in order to further develop advocacy. Think-tank capabilities are also vital to enable the advocacy agenda. Such capabilities include the development of credible and insightful industry-relevant reports, and appropriate data content generation.

Thought Leadership

One early objective of the GPCA had been to develop a reliable, accurate information and knowledge base ("content," or data) for the industry.

In view of the limited internal resources, the GPCA's deliverables in this field were limited to the following:

- The GPCA engaged Nexant-ChemSystems in 2007 to produce a series of three annual reports during the years 2007–2009 entitled the *Gulf Petrochemical Industry Survey Update*. Each of the reports provided members with information on key products, including forecasts for production, capacity, profitability, competitive position, supply and demand, and technology trends.

- The GPCA collaborated with McKinsey and Company to produce a report entitled *Chemicals in the Middle East 2020—Local Opportunities and Globa Implications*. A key finding of the study was presented by Florian Budde during the third GPCA Annual Forum on 4 December 2008.

- The GPCA collaborated with a Singapore-based firm, JDW Technologies, to develop the *Gulf Petrochemicals and Chemicals Directory*, which was published from 2008 through 2010. Later on, in 2012, the Annual Directory was relaunched with content developed in-house.

After 2009, with regard to contributing to the knowledge of its members, the GPCA delivered the following types of report:

Cobranded Reports

In 2010, two reports were developed in collaboration with A. T. Kearney. In the following year, the number of cobranded reports increased to five, two of which were developed in collaboration with A. T. Kearney, one with Booz and Company, one with KPMG, and one with Stratley. In 2012, the number of cobranded reports was also five: four with A. T. Kearney and one with Booz and Company, among which was the first Arabic cobranded report on the GCC Railway and its impact on the petrochemical industry. In 2013, the GPCA released five more cobranded reports.

Internally Developed Reports

In 2011, the GPCA engaged a freelancer to assist in developing a report on the supply-chain industry landscape. The year 2012 witnessed the release of two publications developed using internal resources: the first Annual Statistical Report, titled *GCC Industry Facts and Figure 2012*, and the *GPCA Membership Directory*. In 2013, the GPCA released three in-house prepared reports.

In 2014, the GPCA continued its drive to expand the number of publications of both the in-house and the cobranded reports as well as the Arabic content, the most important of which was the first GPCA sustainability report released during the first GPCA Sustainability Conference in October 2014. The total number of reports released in 2014 was fifteen. These included industry trend reports, statistical reports, cobranded reports, and periodical publications (*Insight, Gulf Plastics, Annual Report, GPCA—Connecting the Gulf*) (Figure 4).

GPCA reports have dealt with topics from global petrochemical feedstock developments to piracy on the Horn of Africa, and from supply-chain talent management to industry research. These reports routinely provided statistical information and metrics for evaluating performance. Their scope reflects positively on the operation of the GPCA and the growing expectations of its membership. Among the leading publications of 2014 is the GPCA's first sustainability report, *Building a Sustainable Future*.

The GPCA's aim was to bring "focus to problems that face the industry" and to "actively seek legitimate solutions." Building on solid data, the association could now begin to position itself "as the think tank of the industry, its knowledge hub and its meeting place, constantly generating interaction among members." Writing in 2011, Mohamed Al-Mady could already extol the benefits:

FIGURE 4. Growth in Number of GPCA Publications, 2010–2014

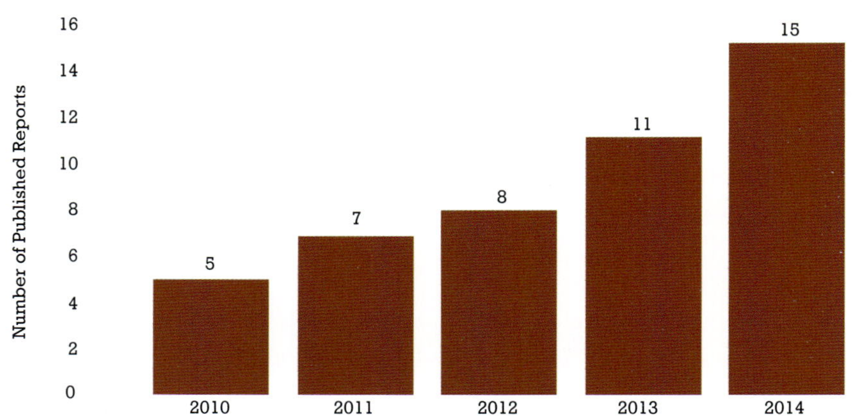

The GPCA's role as a think tank, and its increasingly important position as a provider of real-time industrial knowledge and information, has further enhanced our industry's profile in the global marketplace. Our ongoing industry-relevant studies, reports, and trends analysis have elevated the GPCA as a trustworthy source of information and knowledge throughout the global petrochemical industry.

In addition to publishing reports in both Arabic and English, an important GPCA contribution to content has been the creation of the GCC Petrochemicals Database, which was first launched in May 2012 and updated in 2014. It provides important information about petrochemical products, capacity, production, consumption, import, and export with regard to the Arabian Gulf region and globally.

Through these initiatives, GPCA was increasingly recognized for its important role as a think tank for regional industry, and as the repository of reliable data about the industry and the people who stand behind it. As Hamad Al-Terkait pointed out in 2014, the association's data may be "the most valuable thing about the GPCA."

> We have now a very solid and accurate set of data because the members of GPCA are the manufacturers, and they can send actual and correct figures to GPCA to internally produce reports. It's data about production, safety and also environmental practice, contribution to society, and how chemicals are important. We can use this data with confidence because the manufacturer is giving this report to us. GPCA is representing us. The data is available, in one place, for members to come and collect it. I think this is really the big value.

Advocacy

Even before it was officially founded, the association aimed to be the "voice of the regional industry," one that would "reverberate" around the world. As it worked to build its role as a thought leader, the GPCA endeavored in tandem to further develop its strengths in advocacy. By 2010, as the association grappled with long-term strategy, it was apparent how its role as an advocate for the industry was now of paramount importance.

The GPCA determinedly developed "a clear vision of what kind of advocacy role it should play with regard to the diverse issues facing the industry, as well as a clear vision of its scale of intervention." It took a strong leadership role to develop and articulate an industry position toward governmental policies and regulations on such topics as the environment, health and safety, industry's image, trade regulation in countries importing chemical products from the GCC states, product and production standards, and legal frameworks that encourage partnerships with other industries, such as downstream manufacturing. A key feature of the GPCA's advocacy agenda was its commitment not only to its regional members but to the common interests of all its members, who included many from outside of the Arabian Gulf area.

With regard to such internal issues as regulations related to feedstock allocation and reducing dependence on expatriate workers, the GPCA decided that advocacy would be best carried out by member companies and that the association's role would be to provide data, statistics, analyses, and position papers to support the efforts of individual companies or of the chemical community in a particular country. It would arm members with the tools and information to work with their governments. With regard, however, to trade regulations within the Arabian Gulf region, levels of nationalization, and tax regulations, the GPCA would not play any advocacy role.

By 2013, the GPCA's initiatives had gained considerable prominence and momentum. That year, the association was included in new leadership groups of the ICCA, including its trade policy network group. According to Al-Mady, presence in these key groups was "not only consistent with the association's strategy

The GPCA has developed in a short time into one of the most important associations of the chemical industry, reflecting the shift in gravity of the industry to the Arabian Gulf region. The strengths of the association are its contributions to sustainability, safety, and the environment through the works of its committees, through its publications, and through the many conferences and other events it organizes. The GPCA will play a vital role in the future development of the downstream industry in the Arabian Gulf region.

—*Hubert Puchner, founding board member of GPCA and former CEO of Borouge*

Figure 5. Attendance at GPCA Events, 2009–2014

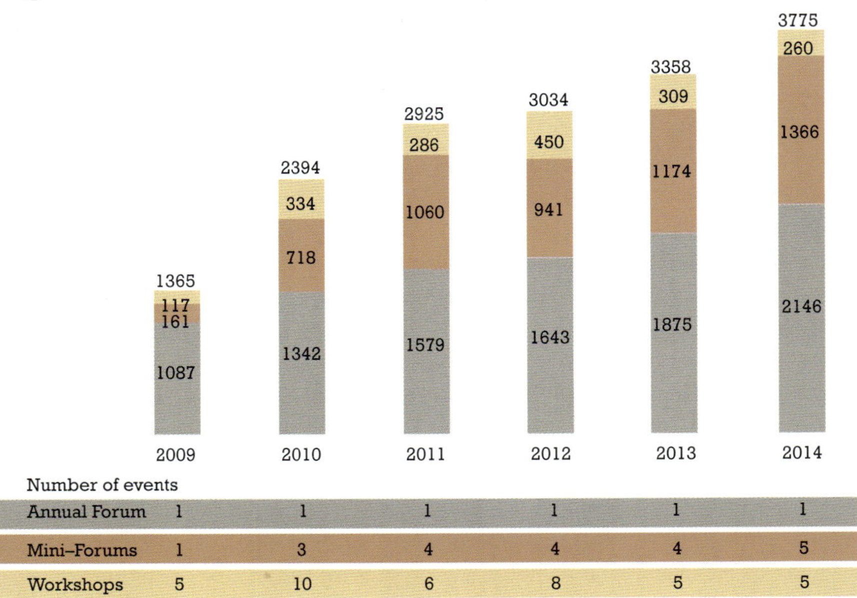

Number of events	2009	2010	2011	2012	2013	2014
Annual Forum	1	1	1	1	1	1
Mini–Forums	1	3	4	4	4	5
Workshops	5	10	6	8	5	5

of advocating best practices and thought leadership, but also a reflection of the growing relevance of the Gulf region to the global chemicals industry."

The GPCA's credibility as the voice of regional industry was further enhanced by its involvement in the Gulf Sustainability and Quality Assessment System (Gulf SQAS), in such high-profile community awareness initiatives as Clean Up the Gulf (later known as the Waste Free Environment Campaign), and in the Plastics Ambassadors Program. It also organized a lively GPCA advocacy roundtable in which petrochemical executives from twenty-five companies, representing all six GCC countries, participated, and signed memoranda of understanding with the European Chemical Transport Association and the Ministry of Environment and Water of the UAE.

Ribbon-cutting ceremony for the newest GPCA office in 2015.

Networking

The GPCA has also built its global reputation by organizing high-quality, attractive networking events. As it refined its strategy from 2010 onward, its leaders saw how its strength in this area could be leveraged to enhance its advocacy work. By assembling outstanding industry experts to address key issues, the association provides excellent platforms for sharing knowledge and discussing issues, trends, and developments that will shape the future of the chemical industry. In 2012, the GPCA organized nineteen such events and saw the participation of more than three thousand delegates in total.

By 2014, the GPCA Annual Forum alone attracted over 2,100 attendees. Other conferences and conventions, including the GPCA's first Research and Innovation Summit, attracted an additional 1,300-plus delegates. Workshops dealing with supply-chain safety, contractor safety, capacity building, intellectual property awareness, and global warming drew in hundreds more. Workshops like these facilitated both the dissemination of information and a stronger understanding of challenges facing the industry.

Through conferences, summits, and other events, the GPCA connects its members with each other and with the global chemical community; it promotes the sharing of information and international dialogue; it serves to influence the future of the global petrochemicals industry (Figure 5).

Moving Ahead

Having refreshed and focused its strategy, the GPCA worked with renewed energy to build upon key themes, such as sustainability, innovation, value creation, operational excellence, growth opportunities, complexity, and the ongoing drive downstream within the regional industry. These themes have played into each other and across specific topics, such as the environment and the supply chain. In 2013 alone, the GPCA launched twelve key publications, manifesting its role as the voice of the regional industry. In 2015, its Waste Free Environment Campaign attracted the participation of over ten thousand people—more than doubling the participation in the previous year.

The GPCA has seen astounding success from its earliest days. In 2010, it embarked on a fresh stage of its continuing journey. The refining of strategy paid off. The GPCA became a full member of the ICCA and in 2013 was awarded a permanent seat on the board of the ICCA, enhancing its role as the voice of the industry of the GCC countries and giving it more leverage in international policy debates.

Looking to the future, the GPCA intends to build on its achievements and to serve as the global voice of the industry in the Arabian Gulf for many years to come.

Milestones: The GPCA's Journey

March 2006: Eight founding members sign a memorandum of understanding, establishing the GPCA. Mohamed Al-Mady is appointed chairman; Hamad Al-Terkait, vice chairman; Hubert Puchner, treasurer; and Abdullah Al-Hagbani, secretary general.

July 2006: The GPCA opens an office in Dubai on Sheikh Zayed Road.

August 2006: The GPCA website debuts.

December 2006: The first GPCA Annual Forum is held, attracting 460 delegates.

March 2007: A Human Resources Committee is established to enable development and cultivation of talent in the GCC countries.

May 2007: The Safety, Health, and Environment Committee is formed, spurring the GPCA's commitment to Responsible Care.

June 2007: The GPCA holds its first awareness workshop on performance management.

November 2007: The GPCA's online database debuts.

December 2007: The GPCA membership count surpasses a hundred. The GPCA also publishes its first directory.

July 2008: The Supply Chain and Plastics Committees are formed.

March 2009: The board elects to retain Mohamed Al-Mady as chairman and Hamad Al-Terkait as vice chairman, while adding six more seats, expanding the board from nine to fifteen members.

April 2009: Abdulwahab Al-Sadoun succeeds Abdullah Al-Hagbani as secretary general.

August 2009: The GPCA board establishes the Advocacy Committee to challenge protectionist measures in key export markets.

October 2009: The GPCA Supply Chain Conference is inaugurated in Bahrain.

December 2009: The Fertilizer Committee is created. GPCA's board unanimously endorses the implementation of Responsible Care.

January 2010: The Communication Advisory Board is formed.

June 2010: The first GPCA Plastics Summit takes place in Dubai.

September 2010: The first GPCA Fertilizer Convention takes place in Dubai.

December 2010: The GPCA relocates to a larger space in Aspect Towers, Business Bay, Dubai, and applies for observer status with the International Chemical Companies Association.

April 2011: The GPCA Plastic Innovation Awards debut.

October 2011: The GPCA organizes its first talent convention in Dubai.

March 2012: The GPCA board retains Mohamed Al-Mady as chairman and elects Rashed Al Shamsi as vice chairman.

June 2012: The GPCA board endorses a new strategy formulated by A. T. Kearney. It also dissolves the Human Resources Committee and replaces it with the Research and Innovation Committee, while the Advocacy Committee is renamed the International Trade Committee.

September 2012: The ICCA board approves GPCA's membership.

February 2013: The GPCA launches the "Clean Up the Gulf" Campaign.

December 2013: The GPCA adds the Sustainability Conference to its portfolio of events.

March 2014: The GPCA hosts its first Research and Innovation Summit.

March 2015: The GPCA opens new headquarters at Vision Tower, Business Bay, Dubai. Rashed Saud Al Shamsi is elected GPCA chairman, succeeding Mohamed Al-Mady, and Yousef Al-Benyan is elected as vice chairman.

October 2015: The GPCA holds its first Responsible Care Conference and Awards.

November 2015: The GPCA hosts its milestone tenth Annual Forum.

March 2016: The GPCA celebrates its ten-year anniversary.

A Note on Sources

This volume is based upon archival materials held at the GPCA, while also drawing on the association's many publications, especially its annual reports and its newsletter, *Insights*. Other important published sources were the *Middle East Economic Digest*, *IHS Chemical Week*, and *ICIS Chemical Business*.

Also of especial value were one-on-one interviews with pioneers of the GPCA, including Mohamed Al-Azdi, Moayyed Al-Qurtas, Sa'ad Al-Shuwaib, Hamad Al-Terkait, Maha Mulla Hussain, Abdulrahman Jawahery, and Hubert Puchner, and with GPCA board member Mohammad Husain. Abdullah Al-Hagbani, Peter Cella, James Gallogly, and Bhavesh (Bob) Patel graciously provided thoughtful written comments on the evolution of the GPCA.